Practical Skills in Rational Emotive Behaviour Therapy

Professor Windy Dryden
Goldsmiths College, University of London

Other titles in this series

Preparing for Client Change in Rational Emotive Behaviour Therapy

Facilitating Client Change in Rational Emotive Behaviour Therapy

Windy Dryden

W

Whurr Publishers Ltd
London

England

...ation may be reproduced,
...d in any form or by any
means, electronic, mechanical, photocopying, recording or otherwise,
without the prior permission of Whurr Publishers Limited.

This publication is sold subject to the conditions that it shall not, by
way of trade or otherwise, be lent, resold, hired out, or otherwise
circulated without the publisher's prior consent in any form of binding
or cover other than that in which it is published and without a similar
condition including this condition being imposed upon any
subsequent purchaser.

British Library Cataloguing-in-Publication Data
A catalogue record for this book is available from the
British Library

ISBN 1-897635-32-X

Printed and bound in the UK by Athenaeum Press Ltd, Gateshead, Tyne & Wear

Contents

Module 12   132

Reviewing Homework Assignments

Introduction

This is the second volume in the 'Practical Skills in Rational Emotive Behaviour Therapy Series'. The purpose of this series is to provide training material for beginning trainees in REBT. A major feature of the series is that I have provided actual and constructed dialogue between myself and my clients to demonstrate the skills that I discuss in the main body of the text. Client permission has been obtained for this purpose and all identifying material has been removed.

In this volume, I concentrate on the skills that you will need to facilitate client change in REBT. Thus, I have included modules on (i) teaching clients the REBT view of therapeutic change so that they can understand the process of REBT and their role within this process; (ii) goal-setting; (iii) eliciting commitment to change from your clients; and (iv) negotiating and reviewing homework assignments. In addition, I devote seven modules to disputing which is a core skill in REBT. Let me repeat something that I stressed in the first volume in this series. No book on REBT can serve as a substitute for training in the approach. Thus, this book and the others in the series are best used as adjuncts to training and supervision. Consequently, I have provided information on where to get training and supervision in REBT in Appendix 3. If you decide to pursue training in REBT, it is my fervent hope that this book and the others in this series help you in your endeavours. Good luck!

Module 1
Teaching The REBT View
Of Therapeutic Change

I have found it useful in my clinical work to explain to clients how therapeutic change occurs, at least as viewed from an REBT perspective. It is possible to do this in many ways and which method you choose will depend on many factors including your client's interest in this subject. Before I outline the steps, let me make a few general comments about this educational issue.

Unit 1: General issues

First, you will probably introduce these steps at different points in the therapeutic process. I have found it most useful to educate the client about each step before he and I do any therapeutic work in the step itself. If you do this, you will help your client to understand what is coming next and you will decrease the chances that your client will be resistant to the work that you plan to do at that point in therapy. It will also help him to engage in the tasks that the therapeutic step calls upon him to carry out.

Another way of explaining what your client needs to do in each step is to do so if the work that you and your client are doing in that step is not going well. One reason for this may be that your client does not understand what is expected of him in that step. If you provide the relevant explanation, then this may help dissolve the impasse. For me, this is a less successful approach than the first approach because the former seeks to prevent the development of problems in therapy, whilst the latter seeks to deal with problems once they have arisen. In a phrase, an ounce of prevention is better than a pound of cure.

Finally, it is possible to teach your client about the entire process of change before you start work on the first step. I prefer not to do this because (i) you will be presenting your client with a lot of information at a time when he may wish to start discussing his problems and (ii) he may not understand what is expected of him and may become unduly confused. However, I have used this approach with several clients who like to see the big picture before they will commit themselves to therapy.

The second point that I want to stress is that educating clients about the REBT change process is a different order of intervention from the specific work that you and your client will be doing in each step. To use an analogy here: when you teach someone the rules of tennis you are engaged in education, whereas when you teach that person the various skills he will need to win the game you are engaged in therapy.

Let me now spell out the steps that clients need to take if they are to effect therapeutic change and show you how to get the salient points over to your client. In this context, note the liberal use I make of analogies. I wish to stress, however, that the analogies I use are illustrative and as you gain experience as an REBT therapist, you will want to develop your own. The following analysis assumes that your client acknowledges that she has a problem which, on balance, she wishes to change and has some idea of how she would like things to be different (see Module 2). Dealing with reluctant clients is outside the scope of this volume.

In discussing the seven steps, I will focus my discussion on what has been called philosophic change. Such change involves a substantial shift in your client's belief system toward greater rationality. There are, as I have shown in Dryden (1995); other forms of change (inferential, environmental and behavioural), but they all involve making various compromises with your preferred REBT strategy of targeting and helping your client to change her irrational beliefs (see Dryden, 1987, for a fuller discussion of compromises in REBT).

Unit 2: Step 1. Acknowledging the general principle of emotional responsibility

The first step that your client needs to take in order to embark upon therapeutic change is to acknowledge that she is largely (but not exclusively) responsible for creating her own emotions and her psychological disturbance. Unless your client acknowledges this, then it is unlikely that she will derive much lasting benefit from REBT or any other approach to psychotherapy come to that. Why? Because she will blame other people and/or life conditions for her problems and will implicitly believe that she can only change if the other people in her life and the conditions that she finds herself in change first. If she holds these views she will have what psychologists call an exclusively external attributional style. Unless you help such a client acknowledge that she is largely (but not exclusively) responsible for her emotions in general and her problems in particular, then either therapy will not get off the ground or you will both be working at cross-purposes.

How, then, do you help such clients begin to accept the general principle of emotional responsibility and to realise that she largely (but not exclusively) creates her psychological problems and is therefore largely responsible for her own therapeutic change process? One way is to use the 'hundred people technique'. Let me illustrate this technique.

The hundred people technique

Windy: So, Mary. You're saying that your boss makes you angry and that's the end of it. Is that right?

Mary: Exactly.

Windy: Well, let's see. Imagine that a hundred women, your age, background and intelligence level all worked for your boss — separately of course — but they all worked for your boss at one time or another. Imagine too that he behaves equally obnoxiously to them as he does towards you. Now would all one hundred women feel the same way about him as you do?

Mary: Well, most would.

Windy: Maybe, but would they ALL?

Mary: I guess not.

Windy: That's right. Many, as you say, would be angry, some would be annoyed, some would feel guilty...

Mary: Guilty? You mean some women would actually feel guilty about that son of a bitch?

Windy: Oh yes. What would they have to think to feel guilty?

Mary: Beats me.

Windy: Well wouldn't they have to think something like: 'It's my fault he's so nasty. I've done something very wrong which proves that I'm a bad person?'

Mary: I suppose they would. I've never thought about it like that.

Windy: And by the same token, wouldn't some of these women be annoyed, but not furious about his lousy behaviour?

Mary: I guess they would.

Windy: What do you think they would have to think in order to be annoyed, but not furious about the way he behaves?

Mary: Something like, 'I don't like it but that's the way he is. Tough!'

Windy: That's probably very true. Now strange as it may seem one or two of these women will even feel pleased about the way he treats them. Do you know why?

Mary: No, why?

Windy: Well, what would they have to think about his bad behaviour to feel pleased about it?

Mary: It's good that he is treating me badly?

Windy: Right.

Mary: But, come now. Who in her right mind will be pleased about such bad behaviour?

Windy: Well, the person may not be in her right mind. But I can think of at least one non-crazy reason why a woman may feel pleased about being treated so badly.

Mary:....(long pause)...well I can't think of any. Put me out of my misery. I'm dying to know.

Windy: Well what if she thought something like: 'I hope he continues because if he does I'm going to report him to his superior. That'll get him into trouble.'

Mary: You're right!

Windy: Now note, Mary, that by saying this I'm not condoning his bad behaviour. If you're right and from the evidence you've given me, I've got no reason to doubt it, his behaviour does stink and is bound to have some influence on how you will feel, but from what we've just discussed do you think that he makes you feel angry?

Mary: No. I can see what you mean. I'm glad that you said that his behaviour does have some bearing, otherwise I would have thought you were saying that my feelings had nothing to do with him and I certainly wouldn't have bought that...

[This is a common client misconception that you need to keep your eyes and ears open for. Namely: 'If you say that my boss doesn't make me angry then you are saying that he has nothing to do with it; it's all me.' To counteract this tendency it is important to stress, as I did with Mary, that the behaviour of others and/or environmental conditions do CONTRIBUTE to your client's disturbed feelings, but they do not CAUSE these feelings. Rather, it is the client's way of thinking about the event that is often the most important factor to consider.]

...but as you've acknowledged that he has something to do with it, I can see that the different ways people think about the same event have quite an influence on the way they feel about it.

Now, of course, the client's last statement is not quite true. You will recall from the first book in this series (Dryden, 1995) that a person disturbs herself at C about the most relevant (for her) part of the A. As I discussed in that book, this is called the critical A and is often inferential. Thus, strictly speaking, the hundred women in the above example are not all evaluating the same event. They are evaluating their critical A's. It is for this reason that the 'hundred people' technique is NOT a good way of teaching the ABC's of REBT. However, please remember that you are NOT teaching the specific role that rational and irrational beliefs have on people's negative emotions at this point. I call this the SPECIFIC principle of emotional responsibility which is step 3 of the REBT therapeutic change framework. Here, you are making the general point that people need to take responsibility for the way they think about events. I call this the GENERAL principle of emotional responsibility.

In other words you are concerned here with emphasising the general point: 'You feel the way you think' and not the specific REBT point: 'You disturb yourself largely by your irrational beliefs'. That point comes later. However, I should stress that there are a number of REBT therapists who would rather teach the specific REBT point first and would thus dispense with the more general point, i.e.: 'You feel the way you think'. These REBT therapists argue that because the specific point: 'You disturb yourself largely by your irrational beliefs' is the core of the REBT model AND that by using it first you can also teach your client the principle of emotional responsibility, then teaching the general principle of emotional responsibility is a redundant exercise. I tend to be in this latter camp myself. However, as you will need to teach some of your clients the general principle of emotional responsibility, you will need to learn some of the methods outlined in this section. Having made this point, let me outline another way of teaching this general principle.

Using diagrams

A good way of teaching your client the general principle of emotional responsibility is by using diagrams. In Figure 1.1 I outline what might be called the general principle of emotional irresponsibility in that the client is claiming that A (a situation) can directly cause her feelings at C.

The diagram in Figure 1.2, on the other hand, represents the general principle of emotional responsibility that I am suggesting that you teach your clients. It shows that it is the person's beliefs about the existing negative event that are largely responsible for the person's disturbed feelings.

As a training exercise, pair up with a trainee colleague and have him/her play the role of a client who believes that 'A causes C'. Using the diagrams outlined in Figures 1.1 and 1.2, help your 'client' understand

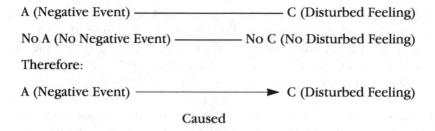

Figure 1.1. Argument used to justify 'A causes C' model.

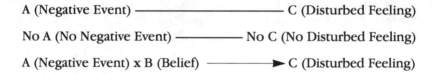

Figure 1.2. A × B→C explanation.

that a more accurate representation is that shown in Figure 1.2. Tape record the dialogue and play the tape to your REBT trainer or supervisor for feedback.

Two common client objections to the general principle of emotional responsibility

As you will soon discover, some clients find it difficult to accept the general principle of emotional responsibility. Your clients will come up with several objections, but here I will concentrate on the two most common: (a) 'But I would not have felt that way if the event didn't happen' and (b) 'If I accept the general principle of emotional responsibility, then I will blame myself.'

(a) 'But I would not have felt that way if the event didn't happen'

Here is an example of how to deal with this argument. Let's suppose that Susan has made this objection in the course of a therapy session. This is how I would have responded.

Susan: Well, that's all well and good, but if my mother didn't interfere in my life, I wouldn't get angry. Therefore, she makes me feel angry.

Windy: Can I put your argument on the white board and show you an alternative view?

[You will recall from Volume 1 in this series (Dryden, 1995) that I advocate asking your client for permission before proceeding with an explanation.]

Susan: OK.

Windy: Correct me if I've got you wrong, but your argument seems to be as follows....(writes diagram on the whiteboard; see Figure 1.3). You recognise that you are angry when your mother interferes in your life. Right?

Susan: Correct.

Windy: Then you recognise that when your mother does not interfere in your life you have no need to be angry. Is that right?

Susan: Right.

Windy: As a result you conclude that your mother's interference makes you angry. Have I understood your argument?

Susan: Yes, that's it.

Windy: Now can I offer you an alternative view? [Again I ask for permission to proceed.]

Susan: OK.

Windy: This view recognises that you are angry when your mother interferes in your life. It also notes that when she doesn't interfere in your life you have no need to be angry. So far this model is the same as yours. Can you see that?

Susan: Yes I can.

Windy: Now. I want you to imagine a number of scenarios. Some will sound a bit strange, but there is an important point to be made, so please bear with me. OK?

[Note that I have prepared the client in advance for the 'strangeness' of some of the scenarios, thus making it less likely that she will find them strange than if I had not so prepared her. Again, I stressed this point in Volume 1 (Dryden, 1995).]

Susan: OK.

Windy: Now how would you feel about your mother's interference if

A (Mother's interference)——————————————— C (Anger)

No A (No interference from mother) ——————— C (No Anger)

Therefore:

A (Mother's interference) ————————————-> C (Anger)

Caused

Figure 1.3. Susan's argument used to justify 'Mother made me angry'.

you had sad thoughts about her behaviour?

Susan...(pause)...I guess I'd feel sad.

Windy: Let me write that up on the whiteboard. Now, how would you feel if you had guilty thoughts about her interference?

Susan: Guilty.

Windy: (writes the client's last response on the board). Now I know this is going to sound strange, but how would you feel if you had happy thoughts about her behaviour?

Susan: (laughs) I'd feel happy.

Windy: (writes that on the board). Now, how would you feel if you had angry thoughts about you mother's interfering behaviour?

Susan: Angry.

Windy: (writes that on the board). Now. here's the $64 000 dollar question. Does your mother's interference make you angry directly, or does your anger stem from your angry thoughts about her behaviour?

Susan: I see what you mean. Put like that, my anger stems from my angry thoughts about her interfering behaviour.

Windy: That's right. Her interfering behaviour contributes to your anger by triggering your angry thoughts; but your angry feelings largely stem from your angry thoughts. (This is shown in Figure 1.4).

(b) 'If I accept the general principle of emotional responsibility, then I will blame myself.'

Some clients will resist accepting the point that they are largely responsible for disturbing themselves because they would blame themselves. For such clients responsibility is equivalent to blame. This is how I generally deal with this issue.

A (Mother's interference) ——————————————— C (Anger)

No A (No interference from mother) ——————— C (No anger)

A (Mother's interference) x Sad thoughts (B) = C (Sadness)

A (Mother's interference) x Guilty thoughts (B) = C (Guilt)

A (Mother's interference) x Happy thoughts (B) = C (Happiness)

Therefore:

A (Mother's interference) x Angry thoughts (B) = C (Anger)

Figure 1.4. Argument used to explain that Susan's anger (C) stems from B (her angry thoughts).

Susan: You say they I am largely responsible for my anger about my mother's interference. But if I accept that then that means that I'm to blame for my anger, doesn't it?

Windy: No. There is an important distinction to be made between responsibility and blame. Responsibility here means that you largely make yourself angry about your mother because you have angry thoughts about the way she interferes in your life. These thoughts are your thoughts and no one else's. Given that you have ownership of these thoughts you can be said to be responsible for them. However, I employ the term responsibility (as distinct from blame) to include the following beliefs: (i) I wish that I didn't have angry thoughts about my mother, but there's no universal law that states that I must not have them. I have them and unfortunately all the conditions are in place for me to have them and (ii) I am a fallible human being and not a bad person for having angry thoughts about my mother. Blame involves ownership of your angry thoughts plus a very different set of beliefs, namely: (i) I (in the case of self-blame) absolutely should not have angry thoughts about my mother and (ii) I am a bad person for having such thoughts towards her. Have I made myself clear?

Susan : I think so.

Windy: Can you put it into your own words so I can see if I have explained the difference clearly?

Susan: Well, you seem to be saying that responsibility is something which is down to you, but which you don't blame yourself for and blame is the same thing down to you which you do blame yourself for.

Windy: That's exactly the point. Let me put that on the board to reinforce the difference (see Figure 1.5). Now, often people are reluctant to take responsibility for what is down to them because they would blame themselves if they did so. They confuse responsibility and blame.

Susan: I did at the start, but you've helped me to see the difference.

Figure 1.6 presents the general difference between responsibility and blame more formally.

Responsibility = What's down to you (angry thoughts) + preferences and self-acceptance

Blame = What's down to you (angry thoughts) + musts and self-downing

Figure 1.5. The difference between responsibility and blame in Susan's case.

> Responsibility = Acknowledged ownership of what is in one's con-
>   trol + preferences and self-acceptance
> Blame = Acknowledged ownership of what is in one's control +
>   musts and self-downing

Figure 1.6. The difference between responsibility and blame.

Having considered how to teach clients the general principle of emotional responsibility we can now go on to the second step of therapeutic change.

Unit 3: Step 2. Recognising that one can effect change in one's psychological problems

Unless your client acknowledges that she is able to effect change in the problem that she has taken responsibility for in step 1, then it is unlikely that she will proceed much further in therapy. In the above section I mentioned two common blocks to clients taking responsibility for their problems: (i) believing that an event causes one's problems because one does not feel disturbed in the absence of that event and (ii) blaming oneself for having the problem for which one is responsible. Other clients will resist accepting the point that they are largely responsible for disturbing themselves because they think that they cannot change. As such this obstacle touches at the heart of step 2: encouraging your client to see that she can change and that she is not a hopeless case. Here are some examples of how I generally deal with clients who believe that they cannot change and that therefore they are a hopeless case. I will again present examples where the client is reluctant to accept responsibility for her problem because this is where the belief that one cannot change becomes particularly manifest.

Example 1: Change is possible — the general argument

In the first example, I employ a general instance where change occurs. It is useful to select an issue where change is particularly difficult, but still possible to achieve. If you choose an issue which the client perceives is easier to overcome than she does her particular problem, then she may say something like: 'Yes, but that is an easy problem to deal with compared with mine.' The implication here is that change is possible on easy issues, but not on difficult issues like hers. It is for this reason that you should select an issue that the client is likely to see as more difficult to overcome than her own. In effect, your aim is to help your client conclude: 'If they can overcome this difficult problem, then perhaps I can overcome my (less difficult) problem.'

Susan: You say they I am largely responsible for my anger about my mother's interference. But if I accept that then that means that I can't change.

Windy: Why not?

Susan: Well, I've always gotten angry with her when she's interfered in my life; therefore, I always will.

Windy: So you believe that because you have always made yourself angry with your mother, you're doomed to continue to do so. In other words, you have no choice in the matter. Is that right?

Susan: Well, yes.

Windy: Do you know any instances where people have changed long-standing patterns?

Susan: No.

Windy: Do people ever get over alcoholism or overcome longstanding addictions to drugs?

Susan: I guess so.

Windy: Do you think it is easier to break an addiction to drugs or to get over your anger about your mother's interference?

Susan: (laughing) ... I see your point.

Windy: What's my point?

Susan: That I may think that I can't change, but that doesn't mean that I can't.

Windy: Good. Indeed, the more you think you can't change the more you will make that statement come true, because you won't do anything to effect a change.

Example 2: Change is possible — the specific inspirational argument

Here, you choose a specific example where a given individual, preferably well known, has effected change in his or her life. Again it is important to choose an example where the person has overcome a more difficult problem than your client's problem, otherwise the client may dismiss the example as trivial and of no relevance to his or her 'very difficult' problem. For some clients, it helps if the example you choose is inspirational in nature in the sense that it encourages the client to conclude, 'If she or he can do it, so can I.' However, other clients are put off by so-called inspirational examples and are more responsive to non-inspirational examples.

Susan: You say that I am largely responsible for my anger about my mother's interference. But if I accept that then it means that I can't change.

Windy: Why not?

Susan: Well, I've always gotten angry with her when she's interfered in my life; therefore, I always will.

Windy: So you believe that because you have always made yourself angry with your mother, you're doomed to continue to do so. In other words, you have no choice in the matter. Is that right?

Susan: Well, yes.

Windy: Have you ever heard of Jimmy Boyle?

Susan: The name's familiar, but I can't place it.

Windy: Well, he grew up in Glasgow where he had a very deprived childhood and led a life of violent crime for many years until he decided to reform himself whilst in prison for murder. And with the help of a number of people he did just that. He was eventually released from prison and now is well respected as a writer and social commentator. Now do you think that changing your angry feelings will be more difficult for you than the changes Jimmy Boyle brought about in himself?

Susan: I get your point.

Windy: What's my point?

Susan: That I may think that I can't change, but that doesn't mean that I can't.

Windy: Good. Indeed, the more you think you can't change the more you will make that statement come true, because you won't do anything to effect a change.

Example 3: Change is possible — using self-disclosure

Another way to show clients that change is possible is to relate a personal example where you effected change on one of your personal problems. The field is divided over the value of therapist self-disclosure (see Dryden, 1991 and Segal, 1993 for both sides of the argument). However, I and other REBT therapists advocate using self-disclosure with clients unless there are good reasons not to do so. As you will see from the example below, it is important to get your client's permission to provide a personal example before you begin to self-disclose.

Susan: You say they I am largely responsible for my anger about my mother's interference. But if I accept that then that means that I can't change.

Windy: Why not?

Susan: Well, I've always gotten angry with her when she's interfered in my life; therefore, I always will.

Windy: So you believe that because you have always made yourself angry with your mother, you're doomed to continue to do so. In other words, you have no choice in the matter. Is that right?

Susan: Well, yes.

Windy: Would it be helpful if I told you a personal anecdote which is relevant to this issue? It may help you to re-think your position on this issue.

[Again it is important to ask permission here. If you launch into self-disclosure, it may be unproductive in that your client may not value therapist self-disclosure. Also listen carefully to the tone of your client's agreement. Is she definite in her response? If not, explore any doubts first.]

Susan: (firmly) OK.

Windy: You've probably noticed that I have a stammer.

Susan: I have, but it's only a slight one.

Windy: Well it used to be a lot worse. I would avoid talking to people and used to get very anxious about speaking in public. I now go on the radio which I never dreamed I would be able to do. Now I realised I made myself anxious, but do you think I concluded that this meant I would always stammer badly and always be anxious about speaking in public?

Susan: Obviously, not.

Windy: What do you think would have happened if I had concluded that?

Susan: Presumably you wouldn't have even tried to overcome your problem. I get your point.

Windy: What's my point?

Susan: That I may think that I can't change, but that doesn't mean that I can't.

Windy: Good. Indeed, the more you think you can't change the more you will make that statement come true, because you won't do anything to effect a change.

Here are some other reasons that clients give for not being able to change:

* I'm too old to change.
* I'm too weak to change.
* I'm too disturbed to change.
* My family won't allow me to change.
* I don't have the energy to change.
* I've thought this way for too long to change now.

It is important that you are able to challenge these arguments when your client uses them. One good way of doing this is for you to pair up with one of your trainee colleagues and have him/her take the role of a client who holds to each of these positions. Use as many arguments as you can think of to challenge your 'client's' views. Tape record the role plays and play them to your REBT trainer or supervisor for feedback.

Unit 4: Step 3. Acknowledging the specific principle of emotional responsibility

You will recall that I have distinguished between the general and specific principles of emotional responsibility. The general principle states that clients create, to a large (but not exclusive) degree their own psychological disturbances. When you teach this principle (as shown in Unit 2) you keep your explanation of how your client does this fairly vague. Thus you may choose to follow the lead of Epictetus who said that 'People are disturbed not by events, but by their views of events' or you may show your client that his feelings are largely determined by the way he thinks. However, when you teach your client the specific principle of emotional responsibility, which is equivalent to the REBT model of human emotions, it is important that you show him that emotional and behavioural disturbances stem largely from irrational, absolutistic beliefs.

In Volume 1 of this series (Dryden, 1995), I outlined three examples of how to teach your client the central role that irrational beliefs play in his psychological problems and I suggest you re-read these at this point. However, as it is useful to have a number of such methods in your therapeutic armamentarium, let me give you two more. The first is called the Rubber Hammer method, whereas the second example is one that I originated myself, called Dryden's Invitation Technique.

The Rubber Hammer method

The following is an example of how to use the Rubber Hammer method when teaching the specific principle of emotional responsibility.

Windy: So what you're saying, Susan, is that your mother makes you angry.

Susan: That's right. Every time she interferes with my plans she makes me so wild.

Windy: May I offer you an alternative perspective on this point and one which I think will help you to achieve your goal of anger control?

[It is again important to ask your client for permission to present an alternative view. If she grants permission she is also more likely to listen openly to what you have to say than if you proceed without gaining her agreement on this matter.]

Susan: OK.

Windy: This way of explaining it may seem strange, but bear with me if you will. OK?

[Note that I have again sought the client's permission here. Also I have acknowledged myself that the method may seem strange to the client. Doing this, I have found, has the paradoxical effect of making the method seem less bizarre in the client's eyes.]

Susan: OK (laughing warily).

Windy: Now this is a rubber hammer. I'd like you to take it (I pass it to the client who takes it). Now again I'd like you to bear with me. I want you to imagine that my passing you the hammer represents your mother's interference, whereas the hammer represents the belief: 'My mother absolutely must not interfere in my life.' Now hit yourself over the head with it. It won't hurt, I promise.

Susan: (hits herself over the head with the hammer which makes a squeaky noise. The client laughs and says...) That's a relief.

Windy: Now, how will you feel if you believe that your mother absolutely must not interfere in your life?

Susan: Angry.

Windy: That's right. Now let me have the hammer back...(Susan passes me the hammer)...Now once again my passing you the hammer represents your mother's interference in your life, but this time the hammer represents a different belief, namely: 'I'd prefer it if my mother did not interfere in my life, but there's no reason why she must not.' Now, hit yourself over the head again...(the client does so)...How would you feel if you believed that it would be preferable if your mother did not interfere in your life, but that there is no law of the universe which states that she must not do so?

Susan: Well I still wouldn't like it, but I guess I wouldn't be nearly as angry.

Windy: Right, you wouldn't like it. You'd even strongly dislike it, but you wouldn't be angry. You'd be annoyed or even strongly annoyed. Now, note that your mother's interference is the same in both situations. What's different?

Susan: My beliefs.

Windy: Your mother's behaviour contributes to your feelings, but your anger largely stems from your demanding belief, whilst your annoyance stems from your healthy non-demanding preference. Now, I'm not sure I've made myself clear. Can you put into your own words the main point about what I've said?

[Once again it is important to determine whether or not the client has grasped the main point.]

Susan: That my mother doesn't make me angry. I do that, with my demanding belief about her behaviour.

Windy: Correct.

Dryden's Invitation Technique

The 'Invitation Technique' is best used to illustrate the specific principle of emotional responsibility when the client applies to himself the actual or inferred put-down from another person or group of people. Here's how I used it with a client, Bill.

Windy: So, Bill. You felt depressed when your friends laughed at you because you thought they considered you worthless. Have I understood you correctly?

Bill: That's right.

Windy: So who made you depressed?

Bill: They did by considering me to be worthless.

Windy: Can I explain something to you which might help you to see that in a different perspective and help you over your depression?

[Note that I ask for permission to put the alternative view.]

Bill: OK.

Windy: Bear with me for a few minutes if I seem to be going off track and if I seem to be asking a lot of irrelevant questions. I'm not and I think you will understand why in a few moments. OK?

[Here I explain that there is a reason behind my apparent deviation.]

Bill: OK.

Windy: Have you ever been invited to a wedding?

Bill: Yes, I have.

Windy: What did the invitation say?

Bill: It announced the wedding of the couple and invited me to attend.

Windy: Was there a reply card?

Bill: Yes, I think there was.

Windy: What did it say?

Bill: Something like: 'Thank you for inviting me to the wedding. I accept or I decline.

Windy: That's right. You are given a choice. Now, let's put your friends' view of you in the same format. I'm assuming for the moment that they actually considered you to be worthless.

[As I showed you in Dryden (1995), assuming temporarily that the client is correct is a typical REBT strategy.]

It would go something like this: 'We consider Bill to be worthless and invite him to consider himself worthless. RSVP.'

Now, here's what's on the reply card:

'Thank you for your invitation for me to consider myself worthless. I accept or I decline.'

Now Bill, put like that what did you reply in your own head?

Bill: I accept.

Windy: And how did you feel as a result of believing that you were worthless, for that is what the statement 'I'm worthless' is, a belief?

Bill: Depressed.

Windy: How would you have felt if you replied in your head: 'I decline to consider myself worthless' which is a more healthy belief?

Bill: Well. I still wouldn't have liked them laughing at me, but I wouldn't have felt depressed. I would have felt sad or annoyed.

Windy: So who made you depressed – : your friends with their laughter and their invitation for you to consider yourself worthless or your acceptance of that invitation, your belief – : 'Yes, they're right. I am worthless?'

Bill: Put like that, it was my belief, my own acceptance of their put-down in my own head. I'm beginning to see what you mean. I'm mainly responsible for my depression.

Windy: That's right. They contribute to your depression by putting you down, let's assume. But you really depressed yourself by your own self-downing belief.

[Let me stress one point here. On realising that the specific principle of emotional responsibility applies to them and therefore they are largely responsible for making themselves disturbed, a minority of clients will disturb themselves about this. As such it is worthwhile adding a statement like the following.]

Windy: Yes, and you don't have to condemn yourself for doing this because we all do it when we are depressed and anxious, to give but two examples. In a sense, the fact that you mainly depress yourself is good news. Because if you have the power to depress yourself, you also have the power to undepress yourself. Now, let's see if we can figure out together how you can use this latter power to help you undepress yourself about your friends laughing at you.

Unit 5: Step 4. Detecting irrational beliefs and distinguishing them from rational beliefs

According to REBT, irrational beliefs are the core of psychological disturbance and rational beliefs are the core of psychological health (see Dryden, 1995). After acknowledging that psychological disturbance is largely determined by irrational beliefs in step 3 of the change process, it is important that your client learns to detect his or her irrational beliefs and to be able to distinguish them from rational beliefs at step 4. I will deal with these two different but related tasks in turn. First, let me show you three ways of helping your client to detect his irrational beliefs.

Detecting irrational beliefs

1. Give your client the following basic instruction. 'Whenever you have a disturbed feeling like anxiety, depression, anger, hurt, guilt, shame, jealousy or unconstructive envy, do the following:

(a) Write down the letters ABC like this:

A

B

C

(b) Make a note of your disturbed emotion at C.
(c) Ask yourself: 'What am I most disturbed about?' and write down your answer at A.
(d) Finally, look for one or more of the following irrational beliefs: must, awful, I can't stand it and I/he or she/they are no good and write these beliefs under B.

2. A shorter version of this instruction is as follows:

Whenever you feel disturbed look for and write down one or more of the following irrational beliefs: must, awful, I can't stand it and I/he or she/they are no good and say what you were most disturbed about.

In asking your client to do this you hope that he or she will be able to identify a relevant A in reporting his irrational belief. For example, one of my clients recently used this instruction and came up with the belief: 'My sister must ask me how I am when I talk to her on the telephone.' If your client does not report an A, then you can train him or her to do so, by giving him some examples of what you are looking for.

3. Ellis's basic instruction:

If you listen to as many of Albert Ellis's therapy tapes as I have, you will soon become familiar with the following basic instruction that he gives to his clients very early on in therapy to help them to detect their irrational beliefs:

'Whenever you disturb yourself, *cherchez le should, cherchez le must*; look for the should, look for the must.' Sometimes he adds: 'If you find it difficult to find your must, just make a note of what you disturbed yourself about, bring this in and I will help you find it.'

Note that with this instruction, Ellis is deliberately guiding his clients towards detecting their musts. He does not even mention the three other irrational beliefs, namely: awfulising, low frustration tolerance beliefs and self/other downing. This is consistent with Ellis's view, discussed in Dryden (1995) that musts are primary irrational beliefs and that the others are secondary irrational beliefs in that they are derived from the musts.

Distinguishing irrational beliefs from rational beliefs

One major purpose of encouraging your client to detect his irrational beliefs and to be able to distinguish them from his rational beliefs is so that he can dispute them effectively. It is therefore particularly important that your client is able to discriminate carefully between rational and irrational beliefs. Otherwise he may dispute his healthy rational beliefs or other non-disturbing cognitions. Here are some ways whereby you can help him to sharpen his discriminatory powers on this issue.

(a) Teach your client the difference between absolute and non-absolute shoulds. In the mid-1980s, I wrote a paper on language and meaning in REBT where I made the point that it is important to distinguish between words and meanings (see Dryden, 1991). Take the word 'should'. In REBT, we argue that only absolute shoulds are the core of much psychological disturbance. Thus, it is important to help your client to distinguish between absolute shoulds and other forms of the word 'should'. In particular, your client needs to distinguish between absolute shoulds and preferable shoulds. One way of doing this is to encourage him to use the relevant qualifier. Thus, when your client's should is rational, encouraging him to use the phrase 'I preferably should...', for example, and when it is irrational, the phrase 'I absolutely should...' makes the meaning clear. To help your client to understand the non-absolute nature of these shoulds have her say, 'I preferably should be approved by my boss, but he doesn't have to do so.'

However, there are other meanings of the word 'should' which are non-absolute and which your client needs to understand so that he doesn't mistake them for absolute shoulds. In addition to preferable shoulds the following is a list of non-absolute shoulds:

(i) *Recommendatory shoulds*. These shoulds point to what your client recommends to herself or to others e.g. 'You really should go and see the new play at the local theatre.' If your client uses the phrase 'I recommend that you...', then he or she will see the recommendatory meaning of this particular should. To help your client understand the non-absolute nature of these shoulds encourage him or her to say, 'You really should go and see the new play at the local theatre, but there is no reason why you have to do so.'

(ii) *Predictive shoulds*. These shoulds represent your client's predictions about the future, e.g. 'I should pass my driving test tomorrow.' Using the phrase, 'I predict that...', instead of 'I should...' should (I predict!) make the meaning of this 'should' clear. To help your client to understand the non-absolute nature of these shoulds, encourage her to say, 'I should pass my driving test, but there is no law of the universe that states that I must do so.'

(iii) *Ideal shoulds*. These shoulds point to the existence of ideal conditions, e.g. 'People should be nice to one another.' Substituting the phrase, 'In an ideal world, people would...' will probably reveal the ideal nature of such shoulds. To help your client to understand the non-absolute nature of these shoulds, encourage her to say, 'People should be nice to one another, but they obviously don't have to do so.'

(iv) *Empirical shoulds*. These shoulds point to the existence of reality, e.g. 'My mother should interfere in my life.' What this really means is this: 'Because all the conditions exist for my mother to interfere in my life therefore she should do so.' Not surprisingly, your client will not use the empirical should very frequently and needs to be encouraged to do so.

(b) Teach your client the difference between unconditional and conditional musts. Your client will often use the word 'must' in its conditional sense which you and she might mistake for an unconditional must. An unconditional must is, as you know, the one that is the core of much emotional disturbance. If your client, for example, states 'I must pass my exams', how do you both know whether or not this is a disturbance-creating must? There are two major ways of finding out.

(i) *Ask for the consequences of the A (in this case, 'passing my exams') not occurring*. If a must is unconditional, it is likely that your client will give one of the irrational belief derivatives as a reply to your question. For example:

Windy: So you say that you must pass your exam. Is that right?

Peter: That's right.

Windy: And if you don't pass your exams?

Peter: That would be unthinkable.

Windy: Why?

Peter: Because it would prove that I would be a failure.

However, if a must is conditional then the client will give you a negative A in reply. Thus:

Windy: So you say that you must pass your exam. Is that right?

Simon: That's right.

Windy: And if you don't pass your exams?

Simon: Then, I won't get into the law.

[Note that this client's must is really specifying the conditions that have to be met in order for him to achieve the object of his desire. In other words, his true desire is getting into the law and the condition that have to be met for this to happen is 'Passing my exams'.

Also note one very interesting thing about my short interchange with Simon. As his must is conditional and he gives me the negative A ('I won't get into the law') that will result if the conditions ('passing my exams') aren't met, this constitutes the beginning of an inference chain (see Dryden,1995). Given this, I would then say: 'And if you don't get into the law, then what...?']

(ii) *Ask for the meaning about the consequence*. You may find that by just asking for the consequence of the client's violated must you will get a negative A in response even though the must is unconditional and disturbance-creating. This is because 'pure consequence' questions tend to pull negative A responses from clients. One way round this problem is to ask for the meaning of the consequence. I will first demonstrate this approach with a client whose must is unconditional.

Windy: So you say that you must pass your exam. Is that right?

Peter: That's right.

Windy: And if you don't pass your exams, WHAT WOULD THAT MEAN?

[Note that I am asking for the consequence: 'And if you don't pass your exams...' AND for the meaning of the consequence: 'WHAT WOULD THAT MEAN?']

Peter: It would mean that I was a failure.

Now let me demonstrate this with a client whose must is conditional.

Windy: So you say that you must pass your exam. Is that right?

Simon: That's right.

Windy: And if you don't pass your exams, WHAT WOULD THAT MEAN?

Simon: It would mean that I won't get into the law.

Windy: And if you don't get into the law, what would that mean...?

[Again note that I am now doing inference chaining by asking for the client's meaning of the negative inferred A's in his mind (see Dryden, 1995) for more information on this critical A assessment technique.]

(c) Teach your client the difference between awful and very bad. You will have already noted that REBT therapists use particular words in precise ways. You will have also grasped the point that it is important for you to make clear to your client the meaning of these terms (see Dryden, 1988, for a fuller discussion of this important issue).

   Continuing this theme, it is important to help your client understand the difference between the terms 'awful' and 'very bad'. If you recall (see Dryden, 1995), awful (and its synonym 'terrible') means, in REBT theory, more than 100% bad and worse than it absolutely should be. On the other hand, very bad means just that, very bad. This evaluation of badness can be located on a scale ranging from 0% to 99.99% badness. Note, then, that it is not possible to achieve 100% bad; to quote again from Smokey Robinson's mother 'From the time you are born till you ride in the hearse, there's nothing so bad that it couldn't be worse.' Awful, however, exists on a magical scale from 101% badness to infinity.

   The difficulty in explaining this distinction lies in the fact that clients often use the term awful to mean bad or very bad. How, then, do you clarify this difference? Here is one example.

Windy: So you are saying that you feel hurt because you believe it is awful that you were rejected by your boyfriend. Is that right?

Rosemary: Yes.

Windy: Now can I clarify something. By awful do you mean that it is the end of the world or very bad but not the end of the world?

Rosemary: Well it feels as if it is the end of the world. I know it's not, but that's the way it feels.

Windy: And when it feels that way, what do you believe?

Rosemary: That it is the end of the world.

[Note that at this point the client is referring to her feelings. As you are encouraging her to identify her belief then this is a very good way of getting her to do so. Later when you move on to the disputing stage of the change process you will want to show your client that her feelings are not a good guide for judging the rationality of a belief.]

(i) *Pain in the neck hassle vs end of the world horror*. Another good way of helping your client to distinguish between awful and very bad was originated by the late Howard Young who worked with lower-class clients from West Virginia, USA (Dryden, 1989). His approach was to put two categories on a board: 'Pain in the Neck Hassle' and 'End of the World Horror' and have clients assign the event being discussed to one or other category. Whilst this method is valuable, in my experience it is not a good technique to use when the client has experienced a personal tragedy because the client will have a negative reaction to his tragedy being seen as a 'pain in the neck hassle', however great that hassle is. In such situations a different approach is called for.

(ii) *Tragedies aren't awful*. If your client has experienced a personal tragedy such as losing a child or learning that she has an inoperable tumour, then it is important that you go out of your way to empathise with her situation and emphasise that this A is a personal tragedy. For reasons discussed above, do not label it as 'a pain in the neck hassle' or 'something unfortunate'. Call it what it is — a tragedy. However, the rational position is that tragedies are tragic, but not awful. This is so because unfortunately such events do happen and no one is immune from them. Because a tragedy is tragic (but not awful), encourage your client to express strong healthy distress about it and help her to see that when she believes such things as 'this absolutely should not have happened to me', a demand which leads to awfulising, then she is adding emotional disturbance to personal tragedy.

(d) Teach your client the difference between unconditional and conditional self-acceptance. I noted in Volume 1 in this series (Dryden, 1995) that unconditional self-acceptance is a rational, healthy perspective on the self. REBT views the self as an intrinsically fallible, complex, ongoing ever-changing process which defies the ascription of a single global rating. Sometimes, however, when clients believe that they accept themselves, they do so only conditionally. Thus, your client may say that even though she has made a series of errors, she can accept herself as a fallible human being for so doing. However, on further examination, it transpires that your client is only accepting herself because her mistakes were minor and that she would condemn herself if these errors were more serious. Thus, what seems to be a rational belief turns out, on further exploration, to be an irrational belief. In this case, your client is still adhering to the principle of conditional self-acceptance. Unconditional self-acceptance, on the other hand, means accepting oneself as a fallible, complex, ongoing process no matter how serious one's errors.

(e) Help your client to specify his full rational belief. One reason why your client may not be able to differentiate his irrational beliefs from his rational beliefs is that he fails to specify the full version of his rational beliefs. As I mentioned in Dryden (1995), the full version of a rational belief has two components: the assertion of a rational component and the negation of an irrational component. The main reason that I strongly suggest that you help your client to specify the full form of his rational beliefs is that otherwise he may easily change the partial form of his rational to an irrational belief. He will especially tend to do this when his rational belief is strong. Let me now illustrate some of these points; in doing so I will put the full version of the rational belief first. Then I will give the partial version of the rational belief and show how your client may implicitly change this partial rational belief into an irrational belief. I want to stress at the outset that the only reliable way of helping your client to distinguish between irrational beliefs and rational beliefs is by contrasting an irrational belief with the full form of the rational belief. The following examples will help you to see why. If they do not, discuss the examples with your trainee colleagues and/or ask for guidance from your REBT trainer or supervisor.

(i) Distinguishing preferences from absolute musts.

Full preference: 'I would like to do well in my new job, BUT I DON'T HAVE TO DO SO.'

Partial preference: 'I would like to do well in my new job.'

Partial preference changed implicitly into a must: 'I would like to do well in my new job (and therefore I must do so).'

Must: I must do well in my new job.

(ii) Distinguishing anti-awfulising from awfulising beliefs.

Full anti-awfulising belief: 'It would be bad if I did not do well in my new job, BUT IT WOULDN'T BE AWFUL.'

Partial anti-awfulising belief: 'It would be bad if I did not do well in my new job.'

Partial anti-awfulising belief changed implicitly into an awfulising belief: 'It would be bad if I did not do well in my new job (indeed it would not only be bad it would be awful).'

Awfulising belief: 'It would be awful if I did not do well in my new job.'

(iii) Distinguishing high frustration tolerance (HFT) from low frustration tolerance (LFT) beliefs.

Full HFT belief: 'With difficulty I could tolerate not doing well in my new job; HOWEVER, THERE'S NO REASON WHY I COULDN'T STAND IT.'

Partial HFT belief: 'With difficulty I could tolerate not doing well in my new job.'

Partial HFT belief changed implicitly into an LFT belief: 'With difficulty I could tolerate not doing well in my new job (but really this would be too much to stand).'

LFT belief: 'I couldn't stand not doing well in my new job.'

(iv) Distinguishing self-acceptance from self-downing beliefs.

Full self-acceptance belief: 'If I do not well in my new job, I can accept myself as a fallible human being. MY WORTH TO MYSELF DOES NOT CHANGE, NO MATTER HOW WELL OR POORLY I DO AT WORK.'

Partial self-acceptance belief: 'If I do not well in my new job, I can accept myself as a fallible human being.'

Partial self-acceptance belief changed implicitly into a self-downing belief: 'If I do not well in my new job, I can accept myself as a fallible human being (however, I would be more worthy if I did well at work than if I did poorly).'

Self-downing belief: 'If I do not do well in my new job, I am less worthy.'

Having now covered step 4 in some detail, we are ready to move on to the next step.

Unit 6: Step 5. Recognising that one needs to dispute one's irrational beliefs to change them

Disputing irrational beliefs is such a central part of the practice of REBT that a number of researchers have unfortunately equated the entire therapeutic approach with disputing. As I will show you later, REBT is much more than its disputing elements. However, as these elements are so core, it is important that you help your client to understand this step in the process of therapeutic change. Later in this book I will devote a lot of space to disputing as a skill. Here, however, I will consider it as part of your overall task of teaching your client the REBT change process.

(a) Disputing involves asking questions and giving explanations

As you will see later in this book, disputing basically involves the application of two main skills: asking questions and giving explanations. Whilst you could explain this to your client at this point, it is better if you can help him to see this for himself. One way of doing this is to ask your client how he would respond to you if you held a belief that he considered harmful to you. Let me illustrate.

Windy: So you can now see the role that your irrational beliefs play in 'creating' and maintaining your psychological problems and the importance of distinguishing these beliefs from their rational counterparts.

[These are, of course steps 3 and 4 in the REBT change process as described above.]

Now what do you think you need to do with these beliefs?

Jack: Change them.

Windy: How do you think you could do this?

Jack: I don't know. I'm hoping you can tell me.

Windy: Well, let's see if you can answer that question for yourself. This is going to sound strange...

[Note how I prepare the client for what may well seem strange to him.]

...but bear with me, because I think you'll be able to get the answer to your question in a way that will be more memorable than if I told you direct. Will you bear with me?

[Note that I ask permission before proceeding.]

Jack: OK.

Windy: Imagine that our roles were reversed — I was the client and you were my therapist. It transpires that I have a belief about myself that I am worthless because my girlfriend left me. Is that a healthy idea for me to hold?

Jack: No, of course not.

Windy: Is it important for me to change it?

Jack: Undoubtedly.

Windy: So let's start the role play and let's record it so you can hear later which methods you used to help me to change. Remember you're the therapist and I'm your client. I'll start off.

Windy (as client): I'm so depressed. My girlfriend left me and that proves I'm worthless.

Jack (as therapist): Is everyone whose girlfriend leaves them worthless or just you?

Windy: But I don't care about everyone. I'm the one who is depressed and I'm the one who is worthless.

Jack: But just because she left you, how does that prove you are worthless?

Windy: Because I feel in my gut that I am.

Jack: But that feeling proves nothing apart from that you have an emotional pain in the gut. What you are doing is taking a painful event like losing your girlfriend and proving to yourself that this means that you are worthless. But it means nothing of the kind. It means that you are the same person as you were before she left you, but you are now without her.

Windy (as therapist): That was very good, Jack. Now let's play back the tape and review what you did to try and help me re-evaluate my unhelpful belief.

[We then review the tape and I encourage Jack to categorise his responses.]

Windy: So, Jack, how did you try to help me to change my belief?

Jack (as client): Well, I started off by asking you questions and then when it looked as if I wasn't going to get anywhere with my questions, I explained to you why you weren't worthless.

Windy: Now, that's exactly what I plan to do with you. I plan to ask you questions about your irrational beliefs so that you can re-evaluate them. If we get stuck then I'll give you short explanations on important points.

(b) Disputing involves using empirical, logical and pragmatic arguments

As I will show you later in this book (see Module 5), REBT therapists use empirical, logical and pragmatic arguments to help their clients re-evaluate their irrational beliefs. In that module, I will demonstrate how to employ such arguments in the context of your disputing work. My objective here, however, is different. It is to help you to educate your client to understand these arguments before you use them. I will now show you how I use one such method which is based on the idea of embodying these arguments in the person of three different professionals.

Windy: So, Jack, you now know that I will be using a combination of questions and explanations in helping you to re-evaluate your irrational beliefs. In doing so, I will be using three major arguments with you. Do you know what these arguments might be?

Jack: I have no idea at all.

Windy: Most people don't, but it is important that you understand what these arguments are before we start. Now these arguments are based on the approach of three different types of professionals. Each of these categories has a different way of understanding their subject. The three professionals are scientists, philosophers and personal finance consultants. Let's start with scientists. How do scientists go about understanding the world?

Jack: Well, they look for evidence.

Windy: That's right. First, they set up hypotheses based on an underlying theory and then they look for evidence in the world that either strengthens or disconfirms their hypotheses. In REBT we call arguments based on the scientific method empirical arguments and in using them we are basically interested in helping you judge whether or not your irrational beliefs are consistent with reality.

Now let's consider philosophers and here I have in mind philosophers who are particularly concerned with logic. What do they do?

Jack: Well, they're concerned with looking at those funny looking formulas and judging what's logical or not.

Windy: That's right. In REBT we employ logical arguments and in using them we are basically interested in helping you judge whether or not your irrational beliefs are logical.

Finally, let's consider personal finance consultants. What do they do?

Jack: They line their own pockets, selling you bad investments.

Windy: (laughs) So you've met some! OK, what are they supposed to do?

Jack: Those on your side give you advice concerning which investments will be best for you.

Windy: Right, and if you want to invest in something that won't give a good return they use arguments showing you that it isn't in your best interest to make such an investment. In REBT we call these pragmatic arguments and in using them we are basically interested in helping you judge whether or not your irrational beliefs lead to good or bad emotional and behavioural results. So when I dispute your irrational beliefs sometimes I will be acting like a scientist, sometimes like a philosopher interested in logic and sometimes like a personal finance consultant who has your interests at heart. Do you have any questions?

Jack: Is this something that I can do for myself?

Windy: Thanks for reminding me. That's a very important point. Yes indeed, this is something that you can do for yourself. After a while, as we get into the disputing process, you'll find that you will be able to use the empirical, logical and pragmatic arguments with yourself when you are able to identify the irrational beliefs that underpin your disturbed emotions.

(c) Disputing involves weakening irrational beliefs and strengthening rational beliefs

The goals of disputing are twofold: first, to help clients to weaken their conviction in their irrational beliefs and, second, to help them to strengthen their conviction in their rational beliefs. How can you help your client to understand this? I often use the following analogy.

Windy: Do you know what you can realistically expect from disputing?

Jack: No.

Windy: May I use an analogy to explain?

[Note once again that I seek permission before proceeding.]

Jack: OK.

Windy: Imagine that you have grown up believing that the number 13 is bad luck. Being a rational individual you want to overcome this superstition. How would you go about doing that?

Jack: Well I would show myself all the reasons why the superstition is probably false and ...(pause)...

Windy: Well there are really two ideas. The first idea is that 13 is unlucky. You really believe it is true, although you can see it is probably false and you want to change it. The other idea is that 13 is neither unlucky nor lucky. You want to believe this, but at present you don't. Now as you said you can review all the reasons why the idea '13 is unlucky' is probably false...

Jack: Oh, I see. I would also review the reasons why the idea '13 is neither lucky nor unlucky' is probably true.

Windy: Exactly. You can do this using logic and evidence as discussed above. You can do the former just by using your mind, but the latter involves coming into frequent contact with the number 13 and seeing what happens. Now, let's suppose that you do this. What will happen to your degree of conviction in the two ideas?

Jack: Well, I'll gradually stop believing in the idea '13 is unlucky' and gradually start believing in the idea '13 is neither lucky nor unlucky'.

Windy: That is exactly right and this is what happens when you dispute your irrational beliefs. You weaken your conviction in your irrational beliefs and...

Jack: Strengthen my conviction in my rational beliefs. That makes sense. I wouldn't have expected to change my irrational beliefs just like that. (Clicks his fingers to indicate a magical change.)

You have now educated your client in three respects concerning disputing. First you showed that you will be asking questions and giving explanations. Second, you explained the nature of the three main arguments you will be using as part of the disputing process. Finally, you helped him to understand that disputing involves weakening irrational beliefs and strengthening rational beliefs. I will discuss the more technical and strategic aspects of disputing in Modules 5–8. Having prepared your client to understand step 5 of the change process, you are now ready to proceed to step 6.

Unit 7: Step 6. Recognising that one needs to work towards the internalisation of new rational beliefs by employing cognitive, behavioural and emotive methods of change

Clients often come to therapy with a number of implicit ideas about the process. Some believe, for example, that all they have to do is to attend therapy sessions and that something magical or mystical will happen as a result. Others realise that they have to be active in the therapeutic process, but believe that all change occurs within therapy sessions. REBT's response is a tough one for such clients to digest. It argues that there is nothing magical about the process of therapy, that change involves active participation of the client both within and particularly outside counselling sessions and that, generally speaking, the more change you desire the harder you need to work on yourself outside therapy. How do I know that most clients want an easy ride from therapy? Because of their response to the following technique. Try it for yourself and see.

Windy: Now, Jill, let me ask you a few questions concerning your view of therapy. First, would you like to make progress very quickly, moderately quickly or slowly.

Jill: Very quickly.

Windy: Now would you like therapy to be very uncomfortable, moderately uncomfortable or comfortable?

Jill: Comfortable.

Windy: So you want therapy to be a comfortable experience where you make progress very quickly?

Jill: The way you've put it, it sounds unrealistic.

Windy: Why?

Jill: Because things don't work that way.

Windy: How do they work?

Jill: The quicker you want to change the more uncomfortable it will be.

Let me now show you how to deal with a number of issues that are relevant to the process of internalising rational beliefs.

(a) Helping your client to distinguish between intellectual insight and emotional insight

During the process of disputing your client's irrational beliefs, it is likely that she will say something like: 'What you say makes perfect sense to me, but I don't believe it' or ' I see what you're saying in my head, but I don't feel it in my gut.' When your client makes such a statement, she is in effect saying that she has intellectual insight into the rational point you have been making, but she does not have emotional insight into the concept. In a brief but important paper published over thirty years ago, Albert Ellis (1963) considered intellectual insight to be a light, occasionally held conviction in a rational belief which does not have an impact on the person's feelings and behaviour, whereas emotional insight is a strong, frequently held conviction in a rational belief which does make a difference to the way the person feels and acts. How can you get this point over to your client? The following are two examples that I use frequently.

(i) The 'Weed–Flower' Analogy I

Windy: So what you are saying is that whilst you see what I'm saying about not needing your mother-in-law's approval you don't believe it.

Jill: Exactly.

Windy: This is an important point. Will you bear with me while I use another analogy to help you understand the point?

[Once again I ask for my client's permission here, for reasons that you should (hopefully!) recall.]

Jill: OK.

Windy: Do you have a garden?

Jill: I do.

Windy: Are you a keen gardener?

Jill: I wouldn't say I was a keen gardener, but I do a bit.

Windy: Does your garden have any weeds in it?

Jill: Weeds? They're the bane of my life.

Windy: Mine too. How do you control them?

Jill: By digging them out at the roots and putting down weedkiller.

Windy: Right. Do you have flowers in your garden?

Jill: Some.

Windy: After you plant them, do they require any attention?

Jill: Yes, I have to water them and make sure the birds don't get at them.

Windy: Why do you do that?

Jill: Because I want them to grow to their full capacity.

Windy: And if you didn't look after them, what would happen?

Jill: They would have stunted growth or if I neglected them totally they would die.

Windy: That's right. What relevance do you think this has for your rational and irrational beliefs?

Jill: That if I don't dig up or dispute my irrational beliefs, I won't change them and if I don't look after or prove the rationality of my rational beliefs, they won't grow.

Windy: Excellent. Now let me extend this analogy to help you distinguish between intellectual and emotional insight. Let's take the garden situation first. Suppose you know what to do in order to have a nice garden, but you don't do it. What effect would your knowledge alone have on your garden?

Jill: None at all.

Windy: Why's that?

Jill: Because knowledge without action isn't going to water the flowers or uproot the weeds.

Windy: Exactly. That kind of knowledge or what we call intellectual insight in REBT has no impact on action and as you say without action the garden will deteriorate. Now if we apply this point to rational and irrational beliefs, what conclusion do we come to?

Jill: That knowing why a belief is irrational and why another belief is rational won't make a difference unless one acts on that knowledge.

Windy: Good point. Unless you think and act against your irrational beliefs and in ways that are consistent with your rational beliefs, your insight into rational principles will be intellectual; you won't really believe them and thus your knowledge will have little if any impact on your feelings and behaviours. However, what is more likely to happen if you do act on your knowledge that you need to think and act against your irrational beliefs in a way that is consistent with your rational beliefs?

Jill: I am likely to really believe it.

Windy: That's right. Your insight into your rational belief, for example, will be emotional in the sense that you really believe it and that strong conviction will make a real difference to how you feel and act.

(ii) The Tennis Player Analogy I

This analogy makes a similar point to the Weed–Flower Analogy I. In addition, it is particularly useful when you wish to make the point that changing an ingrained habit like irrational thinking involves putting up with and working through an uncomfortable phase of unnaturalness.

Windy: Now, how often do you think you will have to question and change your irrational beliefs before you begin to believe the alternative rational beliefs?

Ian: Quite frequently.

Windy: Why?

Ian: Because I've held my irrational beliefs for a long time.

Windy: That's right. Now let me use an analogy to help you to understand a few important points about change. Is that OK?

Ian: Fine.

Windy: Imagine when you were much younger you wanted to play tennis and had saved up your pocket money for some lessons from a tennis coach. On your way to your first lesson you met your favourite uncle who asked you where you were going and you explained about the tennis lessons. He told you that he could play tennis very well and offered to teach you for nothing. The thought of the free lessons and the idea of all the other things you could do with your pocket money was very enticing to you so you agreed. Over the next six months, your uncle gave you weekly tennis lessons, but unfortunately he taught you incorrectly, but as you were very enthusiastic, you diligently practised the wrong strokes not knowing at that time that you were developing some very bad habits. However, the more you played against other young tennis players, the more defeats you suffered. Later you realised what had happened, so you went to have some tennis lessons from a professional tennis coach. She was able to diagnose your faults and taught and demonstrated how to play the various tennis strokes properly. Now would knowing how to play the correct strokes help to improve your game?

Ian: No, of course not.

Windy: Why not?

Ian: Because I would not have done any practice.

Windy: Right. Now let's suppose that you started to practise the new strokes. Would you be comfortable playing the new strokes?

Ian: Not at all.

Windy: Why not?

Ian: Because I would be accustomed to playing the old, incorrect strokes.

Windy: So it would feel natural to play the old stokes and unnatural to play the new ones.

Ian: Yes.

Windy: But would that unnatural feeling stop you from correcting the stroke when you started to play in the old, incorrect but natural manner?

Ian: No, it wouldn't.

Windy: Now it's the same with changing your irrational beliefs. The next time you fail to master something new the first time you will undoubtedly think that you are a failure. Why do I say undoubtedly here?

Ian: Because that is what I've believed in the past and it's natural for me to think that way.

Windy: That's right. However, if you go against that natural feeling you can detect, dispute and change your belief to a rational belief and keep doing so until...?

Ian: Until the rational belief becomes more natural to me.

Windy: Also the more you act against the old irrational belief and according to the newer rational belief, the more you will be convinced by the new rational belief and the less you will believe the old belief. This is what some people call going from 'head thinking' to 'gut thinking'. What do you understand by these terms?

Ian: 'Head thinking' sounds like it means understanding something in your head, but not truly believing it, whereas 'gut thinking' sounds like it means believing it in your guts.

Windy: That's exactly it. Which type of thinking is likely to change your feelings and actions when you fail to master something the first time?

Ian: 'Gut thinking' obviously.

Windy: Does believing something new in your gut take a lot of practice or does it happen without too much practice?

Ian: No, it sounds like it will take a lot of practice.

Windy: Are you willing to do that practice if it increases your chances of getting over your anxiety about trying new things?

Ian: Yes, I am.

(b) Helping your client to understand the importance of between-session as well as in-session work

Whilst the above methods which help your client distinguish between intellectual and emotional insight imply that she needs to work to effect change between sessions as well as within sessions, it is still important to make this point explicit. I often use an extension of the Tennis Player Analogy to underscore the central role that between-session work has in the REBT change process.

(i) The Tennis Player Analogy II

Windy: Now, let me go back to the tennis analogy for the moment, if I may, to stress another point about the change process. Is that OK?

Ian: Fine.

Windy: Remember that you have decided to go for tennis lessons to correct the bad habits you developed when your uncle taught you all the wrong strokes and you practised them diligently.

Ian: Fine.

Windy: Imagine this scenario. You attend tennis lessons once a week and each lesson lasts for one hour. In the first part of the lesson your coach watches your game, points out your errors and models the correct strokes, whilst in the second half you practise what you have learned with the occasional prompt from your mentor. Now let's suppose that you do no practice in between sessions. What will happen to your tennis game?

Ian: Well, I won't improve.

Windy: Why not?

Ian: That's obvious. I won't improve because I'm not practising what I am learning.

Windy: Yes you are, you're getting in the practice in the second half of the lesson.

Ian: But that's not enough.

Windy: Why not?

Ian: For two reasons. First, in order to become proficient at the skill I need to practise it much more frequently than once a week, particularly when I have first learned that skill.

Windy: And the second reason?

Ian: Well, I need to work extra hard to practise that new skill because my old poor habits are still well ingrained. And once a week practice won't really do anything to change things around.

Windy: What do you need to do then?

Ian: If I can find the time, I'd need to practise once a day rather than once week.

Windy: Now let's apply this to the therapy situation and the practice you need to do to change your irrational beliefs. What do you think the implication of this is for therapy?

Ian: Well, the implication seems to be that if I only practise thinking rationally in this room, then I won't get much benefit from therapy.

Windy: What do you need to do to benefit from therapy, which in this case means making the new rational beliefs your own?

Ian: I need to practise disputing my irrational beliefs and strengthening my rational beliefs fairly frequently.

Windy: Like once a day?

Ian: Like once a day.

After your client has understood that he needs to work fairly frequently if he is to begin to internalise his rational beliefs, you can begin to raise the issue of how much work your client is prepared to do. Note that I did this in a general way at the end of the Tennis Player Analogy II. In the following approach, I seek to encourage my client to commit himself to a specified number of hours of DELIBERATE psychological work. I have stressed the word 'deliberate' here because I do not wish to preclude the client from doing such work at other unplanned times.

(ii) The 168 hour week

Windy: So, Ian, you can see the importance of doing therapy work between sessions otherwise it is unlikely that you will derive much benefit from therapy. Is that right?

Ian: Yes, I can see that.

Windy: Now, let's talk about how much time you are prepared to commit yourself to doing that work on yourself in a planned fashion. Now there are 168 hours in week minus this therapy hour leaving us 167 hours. How many of these hours are you prepared to commit to helping yourself over your emotional problems?

Ian: Let me see. I guess fourteen hours.

[It is important to note that, when you ask the above question in the way that I have done, you will invariably get an unrealistic answer from your client. Very few clients will be prepared to commit as many as ten hours per week to therapy work. Note how I deal with this issue. However, I maintain that helping clients to negotiate downwards on the number of hours they are prepared to work on themselves per week is more effective than helping them to negotiate upwards. This hypothesis awaits empirical enquiry.]

Windy: Are you sure you want to commit yourself to two hours' self-therapy every day given your busy lifestyle?

Ian: No, I guess that is a bit unrealistic.

Windy: What would be more realistic?

Ian: I guess half an hour a day would be possible.

Windy: When in the day would you do this?

Ian: In the morning before work would be possible.

Windy: But don't you jog every morning before going to work?

Ian: That's a point. I'd forgotten about that.

Windy: Given that fact, when would be the best time?

Ian: Well in the week, I think between 7pm and 7.30 pm would be a good time and on weekends between 4 pm and 4.30 pm would be possible.

Windy: Only possible?

Ian: No, definite.

Windy: So. let me recap. You agree to do 30 minutes planned work on yourself a day. In the week that will take place between 7 pm and 7.30 pm and on Saturdays and Sundays between 4 pm and 4.30 pm. Agreed?

Ian: Agreed.

Windy: Let's shake on it.

[As I will discuss further in Module 11, Unit 50, it is important to encourage clients to think carefully about when they are to carry out between-session (or homework) assignments and to commit themselves to do them. Note how I intervened to help Ian make an informed decision and commitment on the issue of planned self-therapy.]

Now can you see that this doesn't stop you from using what you learn here at other times when relevant issues crop up?

Ian: Yes, I can.

(c) Helping your client to see the importance of using cognitive, emotive and behavioural methods of change

Whilst REBT is properly considered to be one of the cognitive-behavioural therapies, it does not neglect emotion in the process of personal change. However, because there is an emphasis on promoting philosophic change in REBT, much time in therapy sessions is spent on its cognitive restructuring aspects. This could lead clients to think that any between-session work that they will be invited to do will be exclusively cognitive in nature. This is far from the case, for REBT argues that clients need to use cognitive (including imaginal) methods, behavioural and emotive methods if they are to internalise a rational philosophy. How might you get this point over to your client? By using the following arguments.

(i) The importance of behavioural methods used in conjunction with cognitive methods

Windy: So, Brian, you can now see that believing that you must not be rejected by a woman that you ask out for a date is irrational and it would be far better for you to believe that it would be undesirable if you were rejected, but there is no law that says that you must not be turned down. Is that right?

Brian: Yes it is.

Windy: You also understand that in order to weaken your irrational belief and strengthen your rational belief you need to do what?

Brian: A lot of work between therapy sessions.

Windy: Right. But the question is what kind of work. Let me outline a number of ways in which you could do this work. I'll outline them all and then you can tell me which way would be most effective. OK?

Brian: OK.

Windy: The first way would be for you to sit at home every night imagining that you are asking women out, picturing them rejecting you and practising your new rational belief to the image of rejection. The second way would be for you to ask women out in reality until you are rejected a number of times. However, while you do so you do not deliberately try to change your irrational beliefs, hoping that the exposure alone will lead to belief change. The third and final way involves the same exposure as I discussed in the second approach, but this time you deliberately show yourself the rational belief. Thus before, during and after any rejection, you show yourself that it is undesirable to be rejected, but there's no reason why you must not be rejected.

Now which of these three methods are likely to be most effective in helping you internalise your new rational philosophy?

Brian: The last.

Windy: Why?

Brian: Because it involves both action and rethinking.

Windy: That's very well put. Now what about the remaining two approaches?

Brian: Well, they have their strengths and weaknesses. The imagery one is good because it gets me to practise the new way of thinking. But it doesn't involve me doing anything. It lacks that immediate punch of being rejected which would be present if it actually happened.

[Brian's point that imagery doesn't provide him with the necessary 'punch' is true for many but certainly not all clients. Clients vary widely according to their ability to imagine critical A's in a vivid fashion.]

Brian (cont.): This approach might be a good preparation for the acting-rethinking approach.

Windy: And that's how it is frequently used. Now, what about the behavioural approach without the rethinking?

Brian: Well, that's good because it gets me actually to go out and ask women out, but if I don't consciously remind myself of the new belief as you said a minute ago, before, during and after the event, I may well go back to my old way of thinking.

Windy: Right, so what do you conclude from all this?

Brian: That the best way to really sink in the new belief is by actually doing what I am afraid of doing while practising the new belief at the same time.

Windy: Right. You can't do this for every problem, but where you can it really is the best approach.

(ii) The importance of emotive force in the change process

Windy: So far, Brian, we've seen that using behavioural and rethinking methods hand in hand is a powerful way to 'sink in' the new belief as you called it. Now there's another important point about the change process that is important in this respect. It's relevant in a number of areas, but I'll just mention one if I may?

Brian: Fine. Go ahead.

Windy: Let me first take the scenario where you actually go out and ask a woman for a date and she rejects you. Is it better to say to yourself in a quiet, weak manner: 'This is undesirable, but there's no reason why she must accept my invitation' or to say to yourself in a very forceful, emotive manner something like: 'THIS IS UNDESIRABLE, BUT THERE'S NO DAMNED REASON WHY SHE HAS TO GO OUT WITH ME!'?

Brian: Definitely the latter.

Windy: Why?

Brian: Because it is powerful and I am more likely to listen to myself. If I'm too meek in what I say to myself, I may not even hear myself and I may go back to my irrational belief.

Windy: That's right. Indeed, it is for this reason that I recommend that people use strong, good old Anglo-Saxon swear words in their head. In the past when you have been anxious about asking women out, did you express your irrational thoughts to yourself in quiet, polite language?

Brian: Not at all. My language would have made a sailor blush!

Windy: That's why I recommend that you use profanity, to get through to yourself and to fight fire with fire. Does that make sense?

Brian: Definitely.

[A number of therapists consider this suggestion controversial. But it is best seen as helping the client to use his or her own language. If your client claims not to use profane language to herself, it is often best to refrain from suggesting that she begins to do so.]

Windy: The point I want to stress here, Brian, is that the more you can engage your emotions in the change process, the better. Going over your new beliefs in a strong and forceful manner is one very good way of doing this.

[I should point out that it is important that your client does, in fact, have intellectual insight into the rational belief before using this approach. If she does not, the use of emotive force won't help her to acquire it.]

(iii) Emotional change often lingers behind behavioural and cognitive change

There is one clinically observed fact about the change process that your client needs to understand fully if she is to persist at working to internalise her new rational beliefs. It is that your client's emotions will change after she has changed the way she acts and after she has begun to change her irrational beliefs. If your client does not appreciate this she may well give up changing her behaviour and beliefs with the predictable result that she will relapse. The reasons why emotions are the last to change are complex, but need to be explained, in simplified form, if your client is to persist at carrying out forceful, cognitive-behavioural assignments without experiencing immediate or even intermediate affective benefit. Here is how I convey this to clients. Note that I normally do so after I have shown them the importance of carrying out such assignments.

Windy: OK, Brian. So far you have seen the importance of carrying out behavioural and rethinking methods at the same time and, if you can, to do this with emotive force. Right?

Brian: Right.

Windy: Now, there's an important point that I want to make in this context. My experience as a therapist has led me to the following conclusion: you will need to keep changing your behaviour and your way of thinking for quite a time before you notice any significant change in your emotions. I wish things were otherwise, but this is what most of my clients report.

Brian: Why should that be the case?

Windy: Well, I'm not entirely sure, but my hunch is as follows. It is fairly easy to change behaviour. I know that you find it difficult asking women out, but you'd do so to save the life of a loved one. Wouldn't you?

Brian: Certainly.

Windy: Now it is also relatively easy to change your self-statements at least at one level. Thus, you can fairly easily tell yourself something like, 'It is undesirable to be rejected, but there's no reason why I must not be rejected.' You won't believe it at first, of course, and you will need to do a lot of rethinking and behavioural change to begin to believe it deeply. Now it is at this stage when your emotions begin to change in a significant way. But you need to do a lot of forceful cognitive and behavioural work first before this happens. Thus, when you begin to get discouraged when your feelings haven't changed even though you are working hard at the cognitive and behavioural levels, what do you need to say to yourself?

Brian: That it's worth persisting because my feelings take longer to change than my behaviours and my thoughts.

Windy: Think of it like this. Imagine that you are going to have a bet on a greyhound race. It is a three-dog race, one dog is called 'Behaviour', one called 'Thinking' and the third is called 'Emotion'. Having read about all three dogs, you decide to put your money on 'Emotion' even though it is a very slow starter indeed. Now, the race gets under way and, true to form, 'Emotion' stays in the trap while 'Behaviour' and 'Thinking' are out there racing around the track. Would you tear up your betting slip and quit?

Brian: No, I wouldn't.

Windy: Why not?

Brian: Because I know that my dog is a notoriously slow starter, so I would hang in there and wait until it decides to get started. I know that it will catch up in the end.

Windy: Excellent reasons. Now that is exactly what I want you to do with your cognitive and behavioural assignments. Keep doing them because your feelings are like the dog called 'Emotion' — slow to get started but, after a while, quick to catch up.

Brian: I'll remember that.

(iv) Therapeutic progress is uneven

Even when your client consistently works hard to challenge irrational beliefs and acts on his rational beliefs, his progress will be uneven. It is important to forewarn your client of this ubiquitous therapeutic phenomenon, otherwise he may well become discouraged and give up working to change himself. How can you get the 'uneven progress' idea over to your client? Here is one way.

The Golf Analogy

Windy: Once your emotions do start to change and you can see that you are making progress, do you think that your rate of progress will be smooth or even?

Brian: I'm not sure.

Windy: Well, let's suppose that you have been learning to play golf and that you have started to feel comfortable playing all the correct shots. Now do you think that the more you continue to practise, the more you will improve?

Brian: Yes, as long as I don't practise morning, noon and night.

Windy: That's a good point, you can spoil your game by too much practice. But within sensible limits...

Brian: Within reasonable limits, the more you practise the more you will improve.

Windy: But do you think that even though the overall curve will be upwards, you will experience downturns along the way?

Brian: Yes, I see what you mean, I would go backwards at times.

Windy: Even professional golfers go through bad patches.

Brian: That's right. I remember reading that this happened to Seve Ballesteros a while back.

Windy: Now do you think that the same will happen in therapy?

Brian: Yes, I suppose that it would.

Windy: So when you practise the skills that you are learning here regularly and steadily outside, your overall curve will be upwards, but...?

Brian: Within that, my progress will be uneven. A matter of two steps forward and one step back.

Windy: And sometimes even one step forward and two back. Now we'll be closely monitoring your progress together and sometimes it will be apparent why you are not going forward. But at other times, there won't be any reason other than 'progress is uneven'.

Brian: That it is a natural part of change.

Windy: You've put that more clearly than I have. Exactly. So when you notice that you are not going forwards or even that you are going backwards despite working steadily on yourself, what could you say to yourself?

Brian: That this is part of the territory of therapy. There may be a specific reason for it in which case we can find it and do something about it. On the other hand, it might be just one of those things which happens from time to time and if I persist, I'll come out of it.

Windy: Now do you find that discouraging or hopeful?

Brian: On the hopeful side, although I can't say I'm jumping up and down with joy about it.

Windy: I'd be very concerned if you did!

(v) Dealing with lapses and relapses

The final point that I want to make with respect to the 'internalisation' process concerns dealing with lapses and relapses. I define a lapse (or a set-back) as a small or moderate return to previous unhealthy functioning, whereas a relapse is a significant return to unhealthy functioning. As I have shown above, small or moderate set-backs are a frequently occurring (and almost inevitable) part of the change process. To the extent that your client is able to deal constructively with lapses, she will help herself significantly to avoid a more significant relapse, as relapses tend to occur when lapses are not dealt with in a healthy manner. The best way to help your client to avoid relapse is to engage in relapse prevention with her. How might you introduce this concept? Here is one example.

Windy: Well, Rachel, you've made quite a lot of progress on overcoming your bulimia and it seems to me that you have made significant inroads into changing your irrational beliefs.

Rachel: I think so too.

Windy: Now there's one issue that I want to raise with you to help you to maintain and extend your progress. OK?

Rachel: OK.

Windy: I want to do two things here. First, I want to help you to develop a list of activating events both external and internal that you would have difficulty dealing with, that if you don't handle well might lead you to binge. Then I want to help you to develop some solid coping strategies underpinned by healthy rational beliefs that you could use in the face of these A's.

Rachel: That sounds like a really good idea.

Windy: After we have done that how would you feel about seeking out some of these situations in graded fashion so that you can practise dealing with them in constructive ways?

Rachel: I don't like the sound of that.

Windy: I didn't think you would. However, it's a bit like having an injection against diphtheria.

Rachel: What do you mean?

Windy: When you are inoculated against a disease like diphtheria, the injection contains a small dose of the disease. Why do you think that is?

Rachel: To mobilise the body's defences to fight against the disease if I encounter it.

Windy: Right. So why do you think that I am asking you to seek out small doses of situations that you are vulnerable to?

Rachel: To mobilise my ability to cope with situations if I encounter them later in full force.

Windy: Now what do you think of the idea?

Rachel: I still don't like it, but it makes sense.

Windy: Will you commit yourself to doing it?

Rachel: Yes.

Windy: Now the second point I want to raise is this. Let's suppose you have a lapse and have a binge–purge episode. How can you turn this into a full-blown relapse?

Rachel: I'm not sure I understand you.

Windy: Well, if you have a lapse as I've described, you can either view that as an unfortunate event which you can learn from or as something that absolutely must not happen in which case you will disturb yourself about it. Which attitude will more likely lead to a relapse?

Rachel: The latter.

Windy: So if you want to stop a lapse turning into a relapse, what do you have to do?

Rachel: Develop a healthy attitude towards it.

Windy: And I'll help you do that.

Unit 8: Step 7. Recognising that one needs to continue the process of challenging irrational beliefs and using multimodal methods of change for the rest of one's life

It would be nice if we could help our clients to eradicate their irrational beliefs entirely but, as Ellis (1976) notes, this is inconsistent with the human condition which is to create demands out of preferences, particularly when these desires are strong. Given this, how can you educate your client concerning the fact that he needs to work at the process of self-therapy for the rest of his life if he is to maintain and enhance his gains? The following is one such way.

The 'Weed–Flower' Analogy II

Windy: Do you know what you can realistically expect from therapy?

Jack: To eliminate my irrational beliefs?

Windy: Well that would be nice, wouldn't it. But that isn't possible. Do you know why?

Jack: No. Tell me.

Windy: Do you remember the 'Weed–Flower' Analogy?

Jack: I do.

Windy: You will remember, then, that in order to control the weeds in the garden you will have to do what?

Jack: Dig them out and put down weedkiller.

Windy: Which is like showing yourself why your irrational beliefs are irrational. What do you have to do to ensure that your flowers thrive?

Jack: Water them and give them the right protection.

Windy: Which is like showing yourself why your rational beliefs are rational. Now will there ever be a time when you can stop weeding your garden and stop tending the flowers?

Jack: No, you will always have to tend your garden.

Windy: Because if you don't?

Jack: Then the flowers won't grow and the weeds will get out of control.

Windy: Right. Now it's the same thing with your beliefs. There will never be a time when your irrational beliefs will be totally eradicated and your rational beliefs will grow without attention.

Jack: So that means that I will always have to do some work on myself.

Windy: That's right.

Jack: I don't care for that.

Windy: Do you clean your teeth, eat and wash every day?

Jack: Of course.

Windy: Why?

Jack: To maintain physical well-being.

Windy: Do you object to doing that?

Jack: No.

Windy: So why object to doing regular work to maintain your mental well-being?

Jack: I see what you mean. That makes really good sense.

Windy: A well-kept garden is easier to keep than a neglected one, but it will always need attention. And a rational mind is easier to keep healthy than an unhealthy one...

Jack: But it will always need attention.

All the analogies I have used in this module have their limitations. As a training exercise, work with a trainee colleague to identify the limitations of any of the analogies that I have used here and practise ways of dealing with these limitations. Have your colleague play a client who criticises your analogy and see if you can develop good counter-arguments. Take any 'client' criticisms that you cannot counter to your REBT trainer or supervisor. Notwithstanding the limitations of analogies, I consider that they nicely show what your client can realistically expect from REBT and they also make clear what he or she has to do to achieve these realistic goals.

Having presented the series of seven therapeutic steps, I will now focus on an important initial stage of facilitating client change: goal-setting and eliciting a commitment to change.

In the following two modules, I will consider two important therapeutic issues. The first concerns effective goal-setting and the second involves you eliciting from your clients a commitment to change. Dealing effectively with these two issues will mean that you will get the REBT change process off on the right foot. Failing to deal with these issues successfully will mean that you will struggle with your clients from the outset.

Module 2
Goal-setting

It is easy sometimes to lose sight of the fact that the purpose of therapy is to help clients achieve their goals. However, it should also not be forgotten that therapists have goals in therapy. Thus, in a seminal book entitled *The Goals of Psychotherapy* (Mahrer, 1967), the book's editor, concluded from his review of the contributions to the book that therapists have two major types of goals: (a) those concerned with the reduction of psychological disturbance and (b) those concerned with the promotion of psychological health. As a therapist, the more you can encourage your client to be explicit about his or her goals and the more you can be explicit about your goals, the better. Doing so will enable the two of you to work cooperatively toward agreed goals. Such cooperative striving towards the achievement of agreed goals is, as Bordin (1979) has argued, an important hallmark of effective therapy.

As I have already argued (see Dryden, 1995), REBT is an approach to psychotherapy that stresses the importance of explicit, open communication between therapist and client. It also recommends that you set goals with your clients. Thus, this therapeutic system encourages you to engage in the very activities that will help promote effective therapeutic change.

In this module, I will deal with goals at three levels. First, I will consider goals in relation to dealing with specific examples of your clients' problems. Then, I will consider goals in relation to your clients' problems as these are broadly conceptualised. Third, I will consider the issue of goals as they relate to the distinction between reducing disturbance and promoting growth.

Unit 9: Setting a goal with a specific example of your client's problem

Let me outline the steps for effective goal-setting in REBT as these relate to specific examples of your client's target problem. As you will see, this is not the simple process it may appear at first sight.

Steps for effective goal-setting

In this section I will outline the steps that you need to take in order to set therapeutic goals with your client with respect to specific examples of his or her target problems. Whilst your client may well have more than one problem, I will deal with the situation where you are working with a given client problem. I want to stress one point at the outset. Whilst I will outline the steps you need to take to elicit your client's goals for change in the sequence that I suggest you carry them out, it is important for you to note that you will more than do so at one point in the therapeutic process. For example, I make an important distinction between the client's DEFINED PROBLEM and his ASSESSED PROBLEM. The defined problem is the way the client sees or defines his or her focal concern, whereas the assessed problem is the same problem put into an ABC format. I argue below that it is important to elicit goals for both the defined problem and the assessed problem but, and this is the point that I want to underscore here, this will be done at different times in the REBT therapeutic process. The work you are likely to do on your client's goal as this relates to the assessed problem will occur later, and sometimes much later than the work you will do eliciting his goal as this relates to the defined problem. Remember this as I deal with the following steps.

Step 1: Ask for a specific example of your client's target problem

The first step in the goal-setting process is to encourage your client to give you a specific example of his or her more general problem. As discussed in Dryden (1995), you can best assess your client's target problem if he or she provides you with a specific example of it because this will help you to identify a specific critical A, a specific unhealthy negative emotion and specific irrational beliefs.

Step 2. Communicate your understanding of the problem from the client's point of view and come to an agreement with him or her on this defined problem

The second step is for you to understand how he or she sees the problem and to communicate this understanding to the client. This is important for two reasons. First, it helps your client to 'feel' understood. Second, knowing how your client sees the problem will help you to assess it using the ABC framework. It is at this point that your basic counselling skills come into play. As you need to convey understanding, the skills of clarification and reflection are particularly useful. In addition, you will need to phrase your attempts at understanding as just that — attempts. As such, there needs to be a tentative quality to your interventions which need to be put as hunches to be confirmed or denied rather than as incontrovertible facts.

For example, it is best to say: 'So, you seem to find it difficult getting down to studying when you know that your friends are out having a good time. Have I understood you correctly', rather than 'You find it difficult getting down to studying when you know that your friends are out having a good time.'

In the former statement, the therapist has phrased the statement in a tentative fashion and has put understanding as a hunch which he or she is testing. This enables the client to correct the therapist if the therapist is off track. In the latter statement, however, the therapist has phrased the statement more definitely and has not checked out his or her understanding of what the client has said, assuming that he or she has got it right. This makes it more difficult for the client to correct the therapist if he or she is off beam.

The purpose of being tentative and testing out one's hunches is that you want to come to an agreed understanding with your client on the problem as he or she sees it. I call this 'coming to an agreement with the client on the DEFINED PROBLEM'. Later in the goal-setting process, you will need to arrive at an agreement with the client on the ASSESSED PROBLEM.

Step 3. Elicit the client's goal with respect to the defined problem

It is useful to elicit the client's goal in relation to the defined problem. Whilst this goal may change once you have assessed the problem, nevertheless it is helpful to learn in which direction your client is thinking with respect to what he or she considers a satisfactory outcome of the problem. Indeed, it is here that you will frequently discover that your client has unrealistic or unobtainable goals for change. If so, you will need to confront this issue. Whether you do so at the point when your client has revealed his unrealistic or unobtainable goal or whether you choose to do so later, you do have to deal with the issue; otherwise, your client will think that you agree with the problematic (i.e. from your perspective) goal when, in fact, you don't. I will discuss how to deal with unrealistic and unobtainable goals in a moment, but first let me show you how you might usefully elicit your client's goal with respect to the defined problem.

Let me use the example that I introduced above. As a reminder the client (whose name is Clare) defined her problem as follows: 'I find it difficult getting down to studying when I know that my friends are out having a good time.'

Here is how I would work with Clare to identify her goal as it relates to this defined problem.

Windy: So you find it difficult getting down to studying when you know your friends are out having a good time. What would you like to achieve from counselling on this issue?

[Alternative questions might include:

(i) What would you like to be able to do instead?
(i) How would you like to change?
(iii) What would be in your best interests to do?]

Clare: To be able to study even when I know my friends are out enjoying themselves.

If Clare replied that she didn't know, I would have employed other techniques such as:

* Imagery: This involves having your client imagine a preferred solution to her problem (e.g. 'Close your eyes and imagine a scene where you are doing what is productive for you even when your friends are out enjoying themselves. What would you be doing in that image?'). Having elicited this preferred scenario, ask the client to give reasons for his choice.
* Time projection: This involves your client projecting himself into the future and stating how she would like to have acted at the time in question (e.g. 'Imagine that we are a year in the future. Looking back, would you rather have studied at the time we are discussing or not?'). Then, ask the client to explain her answer.
* A best friend's suggestion: This involves asking your client to imagine how her best friend would suggests he handle the problem. (e.g. 'Would your best friend suggest that you study even though you know that he and others might be out enjoying themselves? If so, why do think he would say that?'). If you use this technique you need to ensure that your client's best friend does, in fact, have her interests at heart.
* A worst enemy's suggestion: This is the opposite of the best friend's suggestion and is useful in that it helps the person to see that an enemy might be quite happy to see her continue this self-defeating behaviour (e.g. 'What would your worst enemy suggest that you do when you know that your friends are out enjoying themselves and you need to study?'). Explore the client's answer and ask her to set a suitable goal at the end of the exploration.
* Therapist suggested options: If none of the above techniques helps to elicit the client's goals on his defined problem, then you as therapist might provide your client with possible goal options. If you do this, it is very important that you give your client an opportunity to discuss those options with you. Your role here is to encourage him to reflect on the advantages and disadvantages of all the provided options as a way of choosing a relevant goal.

Step 4. Dealing with unrealistic and unobtainable goals

It sometimes transpires when you are working with your client to identify his goals with respect to his or her defined problem that he or she will nominate goals which are unrealistic or unobtainable. As I pointed out earlier, when your client comes up with such a goal you do need to deal with it, but not necessarily at the precise time when your client discloses it. Thus, whilst making a mental or preferably a written note of this goal, you may choose to wait until you have assessed the client's problem and determined his or her goal with regard to the assessed problem. When you decide to confront the client on his or her unrealistic or unobtainable goal must be matter of clinical judgment and I urge you to discuss such matters with your REBT supervisor. What I will do here is to detail the kinds of client goals which are unrealistic or unobtainable. Then, I will give an example of how to deal with the situation where your client nominates an unrealistic or unobtainable goal in relation to his or her defined problem.

What are unrealistic and unobtainable goals?

It would be nice if clients set goals for change that were achievable, realistic and involve them changing some aspect of themselves. Suffice it to say, this does not always occur! The following list contains the unrealistic or unobtainable goals that you will most frequently encounter in REBT.

(a) Changing impersonal negative events

Here your client nominates a goal which involves a change in some aspect of the situation (or A) that he is disturbing himself about. Let's suppose King Canute came to see you for counselling. His complaint is that he is angry because the tide will not obey him and go back when he orders it to do so. You have accurately defined his problem and go on to ask him for his goal. He replies that he wants you to help him to change the tide so that it goes back at his command. Would you accept this as a legitimate therapeutic goal? Of course you wouldn't. You would explain to King Canute that influencing the tide is outside his control despite the fact that he is a king. You would encourage him instead to set as an achievable goal feeling annoyed rather than angry about the grim reality that the tide is not compliant with his wishes.

(b) Changing other people

Suppose your client is depressed because she claims that her boss makes, from her perspective, unreasonable demands on her at work. In response to your enquiry concerning her goal for change, she replies: 'I want my boss to stop making unreasonable demands on me.' If you consider this goal carefully, it points to a change in the other person's behaviour. Now, on the face of it, this may seem quite reasonable. If her boss is making too many demands on the client what is wrong in her wanting him to change? The answer is both nothing and everything. There is nothing wrong with her goal if we treat it as a healthy desire, i.e. it is rational for her to want her boss to change. However, there is everything wrong with this statement as a therapeutic goal.

It is important for you to note and to encourage your client to appreciate that it is not within her power to change her boss. The client can only realistically hope to change what is in her power to change — namely, her thoughts, behaviour, feelings etc. Thus, as she cannot *directly* change her boss, you cannot as her therapist profitably accept this as a legitimate goal. Now, of course, your client can influence her boss to change, and these influence attempts may be successful. This means that it is legitimate to accept as your client's goal changes in her attempts to influence her boss because these new attempts are within her control. Accepting your client's new influence attempts as a legitimate goal for change is very different from accepting a change in her boss's behaviour as a legitimate goal. The former is within the client's control, the latter is not.

(c) Feeling neutral about negative events

It sometimes occurs in REBT that clients indicate that they want to feel neutral about negative events. Consider Geraldine who was rejected by her boyfriend and felt very hurt about this. Here is an excerpt from my therapy with her which illustrates this unrealistic goal and how I responded to it.

Windy: So, Geraldine, the problem as I understand it is that you feel very hurt about Keith ending the relationship. Have I understood you correctly?

Geraldine: Yes you have.

Windy: What would like to achieve from counselling on this issue?

Geraldine: I want not to feel anything about it.

Windy: The only way I can help you do that is to help you to develop the belief: 'I don't care whether Keith ended the relationship or not. It is a matter of indifference to me.' How realistic is it for you to believe that?

Geraldine: Put like that it isn't realistic at all. But it hurts so much I just want an end to the pain.

Windy: I understand that you do feel very hurt about the ending of your relationship with Keith and I do want to help you deal with your hurt. But, I want to do so in a way that is realistic and lasting. The trouble with trying to convince yourself that you don't care when, in fact, you care too much is that it is a lie and you just can't sustain that lie. How about this as an alternative? What if I can help you to feel very disappointed about being rejected rather than very hurt about it? This would mean that you would still care about what happened to you, but you wouldn't care *too* much about it. How does that seem to you as a reasonable goal?

Geraldine: I see what you mean. That would be fine if I could achieve it.

[If Geraldine could not see the difference between hurt and disappointment, I would use a variety of teaching points to clarify this distinction (see Dryden, 1995).]

Windy: If you can see the sense of that then I'll do my best to help you achieve it.

(d) Seeking goals which would perpetuate the client's irrational beliefs

Sometimes clients come up with goals with respect to their defined problems which are within their control, but pursuing these goals would serve to perpetuate their irrational beliefs. Let me give a few examples of what I mean.

(i) Defined problem: I find it difficult getting down to studying when I know that my friends are out having a good time.

Goal: To leave my studies and join my friends whenever they go out without feeling guilty.

This would not be an unrealistic goal if the client was studying for long hours and not taking any breaks from her work. However, in this case the client was procrastinating on her studies and was spending her time watching TV when she knew that her friends were out enjoying themselves. Accepting her goal of joining her friends whenever they went out would perpetuate the irrational beliefs that underpinned her procrastination. Here, you could first establish that studying was in your client's best long-term interests and then help her to plan her time so that she spent enough time studying and some time socialising with her friends.

(ii) Defined problem: I'm depressed because my boss makes unreasonable demands on me at work.

Goal: To tell my boss off whenever he makes unreasonable demands on me.

The problem with this goal is twofold. It does not deal with the issue of the client's depression and it encourages the client to develop a new emotional problem — anger. Thus, if you accept this goal you will be leaving intact the irrational beliefs underpinning her depression and encouraging the development of anger-related irrational beliefs. This is how to proceed. First, encourage your client to consider the benefits of healthy assertion over making anger-based rebukes in the light of what she knows about her boss. Review the material on annoyance vs anger in Dryden (1995) as an aid here. Second, help your client to see that she will need to deal with her depression before she can assert herself adequately with her boss.

(iii) Defined problem: I feel very hurt about Keith ending our relationship.

Goal: To beg Keith to take me back.

Once again this goal does not help the client to tackle her feelings of hurt about the rejection. Indeed, the client is seeking to deal with the rejection by getting rid of it. In doing so, her begging behaviour indicates that she has another problem — a dire need either to have a relationship or a dire need for comfort. Accepting her goal again means that you will bypass her hurt-related irrational beliefs and legitimise whatever irrational beliefs underpin her begging.

(e) Seeking intellectual insight

Rational emotive behaviour therapy distinguishes between two types of insight: intellectual insight and emotional insight (Ellis, 1963). It defines intellectual insight as a light acknowledgment that one's irrational beliefs are inconsistent with reality, illogical and self-defeating and that the rational alternatives to these beliefs are consistent with reality, logical and self-helping. However, such insight does not, by itself, change how one feels and acts, but is seen as an important prelude to emotional insight. This form of insight is defined as a strong conviction that one's irrational beliefs are inconsistent with reality, illogical and self-defeating and that the rational alternatives to these beliefs are consistent with reality, logical and self-helping. Here, though, this strong conviction does affect how the person feels and acts. In short, when a person has intellectual insight, he or she still experiences unhealthy negative emotions and acts in self-defeating ways when faced with negative A's, whereas with emotional insight, he or she responds to these same A's with healthy negative emotions and self-enhancing behaviour.

When a client responds to your enquiry about goals by saying that he or she wants to understand the target problem, he or she often holds the implicit idea that gaining such insight is sufficient for change to occur. Unless this idea is identified and confronted, your client will only make limited gains from REBT. Whilst some clients do seek what may be called 'rational-emotive intellectual insight' in that they are genuinely interested in what the approach has to say about the nature of their problems, most clients in my experience are looking for what may be called 'psychodynamic intellectual insight' in that they hope to identify childhood determinants of their problems which when discovered will lead to problem resolution. It follows from what I have said above that neither rational-emotive nor psychodynamic intellectual insight is sufficient for psychological change to take place.

Explaining to your client that intellectual insight has its place, but is insufficient for change to occur, often helps the client to identify a more functional goal. It also helps the client to distinguish between insight as a therapeutic MEANS and a change in psychological functioning as a therapeutic GOAL. This is demonstrated in the following interchange.

Windy: So you find it difficult getting down to studying when you know your friends are out having a good time. What would you like to achieve from counselling on this issue?

Clare: I'd like to understand why I have this problem.

Windy: What information are you looking for?

Clare: Well, there must be something in my childhood that would explain why I have so much difficulty studying when my friends are out.

Windy: Let's suppose there was. What would you hope having this information would do for you?

Clare: It would help me solve this problem.

Windy: And if your problem was solved what would be different?

Clare: I would be able to study even when I knew that my friends were out enjoying themselves.

[Note that this is Clare's real goal. She hopes that psychodynamic intellectual insight will provide the MEANS whereby this GOAL can be achieved. It is important to distinguish between the means and the goal and this is what I address in my next response.]

Windy: Let me put what you've said a little differently. It sounds to me from what you've said that your goal is to be able to study even when you know that your friends are out enjoying themselves. You hope that the way to achieve this goal is by finding a reason in your childhood.

Have I understood you correctly?

Clare: Yes.

Windy: Well, I'm happy to work with you towards your goal. However in REBT, we have a different view on the best way that people can achieve their therapeutic goals. Let me outline the REBT position on this issue...

[I would then discuss the REBT view of therapeutic change as it pertains to the role of intellectual and emotional insight.]

Step 5. Assess the defined problem using the ABC's of REBT and come to an agreement with him on this assessed problem.

As I have dealt fully with the issue of assessing clients' problems in Module 6 (Dryden 1995), I will make only a few points that are particularly relevant to the topic of goal-setting here. Remember that the emotional C's of clients' problems will generally be unhealthy negative emotions (see Dryden, 1995). However, don't forget that C's can also be behavioural.

It is possible to treat behavioural C's in two ways. First, you can regard behavioural C's as actual expressions of action tendencies that stem from unhealthy negative emotions. In this case you need to target these unhealthy negative emotions for change. Second, you can regard behavioural C's as stemming directly from the client's irrational beliefs and as such they can themselves be targeted for change.

As with the defined problem, it is important to agree with your client that your assessment of his problem is accurate. Doing so will help you to set a healthy goal with respect to the assessed problem. Conversely, failing to make such an agreement will lead to difficulties in goal-setting with respect to the inaccurately assessed target problem.

Step 6. Elicit the client's goal with respect to the assessed problem

If you have accurately assessed the specific example of your client's problem, you will have identified an unhealthy negative emotion and, if relevant, a self-defeating behavioural response at C, a critical A and a set of irrational beliefs at B. The next step is for you to elicit your client's goal which is based on your client's assessed problem. This will be in relation to the critical A and will usually involve a negative healthy emotion and a constructive behavioural response. Let me discuss an example based on an assessment of Clare's defined problem as discussed above (see p. 52). If you recall, her defined problem was: 'I find it difficult getting down to studying when I know that my friends are out having a good time.'

My assessment of this problem revealed the following ABC:

A = The unfairness of being deprived of company when I want it.

B = I must have fairness in my life at the moment.

It's terrible to be deprived in this unfair way.

I can't bear this unfair deprivation.

Poor me!

C = Self-pitying depression and procrastination on studying.

Here is how I helped Clare set a realistic and functional goal with respect to the assessed problem. Note, in particular, that in keeping with REBT theory, I assume temporarily that Clare's inferred A is true (see Dryden, 1995 for the rationale of so doing). Thus, I help her to set an emotional and behavioural goal in light of the 'unfairness' of the situation.

Windy: So, let's assume that you are in an unfair situation; how is your depression helping you to study?

[Note that here I am drawing on Clare's goal with respect to her defined problem, i.e. 'To be able to study even when I know my friends are out enjoying themselves.']

Clare: It's not. In fact, it's discouraging me.

Windy: Right, so what alternative negative emotion will help you to study?

[I deliberately phrased my question in this somewhat oblique way to encourage Clare to think hard about the issue.]

Clare: What NEGATIVE emotion will help me study? I don't understand.

Windy: Well, think about it? You are never going to like the unfairness of the situation, are you?

Clare: No, I guess not.

Windy: Nor are you likely to be indifferent to it, are you?

Clare: No.

Windy: So, what's left?

Clare: To feel negative about it.

Windy: That's right, but there are two different types of negative emotions. There are what I call unhealthy negative emotions which generally inhibit people from adjusting to a negative life event or from taking constructive action to change it and there are healthy negative emotions which are constructive emotional responses to negative life events and do help people to change these events or make a constructive adjustment if the situation cannot be changed. Now, let's take your feelings of depression about the unfair situation where you need to study when your friends are out enjoying themselves. Is your depression a healthy or unhealthy emotional response?

Clare: Clearly it's unhealthy.

Windy: Why?

Clare: Because it doesn't help me to study.

Windy: Right. Now, given that you are faced with what you consider to be an unfair situation, what would be a healthy negative emotional response?

Clare To be disappointed or sad about it.

Windy: Right, now would that be a realistic-feeling goal for you?

Clare: Yes, I think it would be.

Windy: And would it help you to get down to studying when you knew that your friends were out enjoying themselves?

Clare: Yes, I think it would.

Windy: So let me summarise. When you are faced with the unfairness of your friends going out to enjoy themselves, you want to strive to feel sad or disappointed, but not depressed about this and to get down to doing some studying. Is that right?

Clare: Yes.

Windy: OK, let's both make a note of that goal and let's move on to helping you to achieve that goal...

As mentioned above it is also possible to set a goal in respect of the client's assessed problem, where C is just behavioural. This involves you encouraging the client to set a realistic and adaptive behavioural goal in the face of a negative A. In Clare's case this would be: 'I want to get down to studying even when I am faced with unfairness of staying in when I know that my friends are out enjoying themselves.'

Unit 10: Setting a goal with respect to your client's broad problem

Let me begin this section by distinguishing between a broad problem and a specific example of a broad problem. A broad problem tends to be general in nature and probably comprises several different examples. A specific example of a broad problem is just that — one concrete instance of a broad problem comprising several similar examples. For example, Clare's broad problem was 'procrastinating over my studies whenever there is something more attractive to do.' A specific example of Clare's broad problem was the one discussed at length above, namely: 'I find it difficult getting down to studying when I know that my friends are out having a good time.'

Many of the issues that I have just dealt with concerning setting goals with respect to specific examples of your clients' broad problems also emerge when you come to set goals in respect to these broad problems. As such I will not repeat myself. What I will do is to provide an example of one client's broad problems and the goals I set with her on the problems.

Problem	*Goal*
1. Feel anxious about approaching women	1. To feel concerned about approaching women, but not anxious about doing so. To approach them despite feeling concerned
2. Guilty about past wrongdoings	2. To feel remorseful but not guilty about past wrongdoings and make amends where relevant
3. Procrastinate over studies	3. To make a study timetable and keep to it
4. Feel anxious about hosting any kind of gathering in case something goes wrong and therefore avoid being a host	4. To arrange a gathering and feel concerned but not anxious about something going wrong
5. Avoid going to shopping mall because of panic attacks	5. To go to shopping mall and feel concerned but not anxious at first and then to feel comfortable about going after repeated exposure

I want you to note five things about these goals.

(i)   All of the goals are within the client's sphere of influence, i.e. they are all achievable.

(ii)   All of the goals indicate the presence of an emotional and behavioural state. It is important therefore to avoid setting goals with your clients which involve the diminution or absence of a state. Thus, instead of the goal 'to feel less anxious about...' encourage your client to strive 'to feel concerned, but not anxious about...' Similarly, instead of the goal 'not to feel guilty about...' encourage your client 'to feel remorseful, but not guilty about...'

(iii) Most of the goals contain a negative healthy emotion in response to a negative activating event. You will also note that whilst the presence of a healthy negative emotion is clearly stated, the absence of an unhealthy negative emotion is also made explicit.

(iv) All of the goals contain a piece of functional behaviour.

(v) One of the goals (i.e. no. 5) contains an initial healthy negative feeling which then becomes a comfortable feeling state as the result of repeated practice. This last point is important. Whilst it is functional for your client to have a healthy negative emotional response to a negative life event, as a counsellor concerned with your client's long-term well-being, you will want her to attempt to change this negative A and increase the number of positive A's in her life. This brings us to the third issue concerning goal-setting in REBT.

Unit 11: Moving from overcoming disturbance to promoting psychological health

As I mentioned at the beginning of this module, it is possible to think of the goals of psychotherapy as falling into two categories: those to do with overcoming psychological disturbance and those which serve to promote psychological health or growth.

Overcoming disturbance goals (henceforth called OD goals) relates to the problems that clients bring to psychotherapy. Thus, when clients have achieved their OD goals, they experience healthy negative emotions when they confront the negative A's about which they previously disturbed themselves and they are able to take constructive action to try and change these negative events.

Psychological health goals (henceforth called PH goals), on the other hand, are related to a number of broad criteria of mental health which are not situation specific. PH goals, then, generally go well beyond OD goals. Although helping clients towards PH goals is beyond the scope of this book, it is important for you to realise that doing so is a legitimate task for REBT therapists. I outline REBT's view of some of the major criteria of mental health in Figure 2.1 to give you some idea of what helping clients to pursue PH goals might involve for clients (for a fuller discussion of REBT's position on these criteria consult Ellis & Dryden, 1987 and Dryden, 1994a).

In general, you will help your client to work toward her OD goals before raising the issue of PH goals. In my experience most of your clients will wish to terminate therapy once they are have achieved their OD goals. In this respect, Maluccio (1979) found that clients were far more satisfied with what they achieved from therapy on termination than were their therapists. So don't be surprised if most of your clients are not interested in working towards psychological health and don't regard this as a failure on your part if this is the case.

1. Enlightened self-interest

Here the person basically puts herself first and puts the interests of significant others a close second. Sometimes, however, she will put the interests of others before her own. Enlightened self-interest is therefore a flexible position and contrasts with selfishness (the dogmatic position where the person is only concerned with her own interests and is indifferent to the interests of others) and selflessness (the position where the person always puts the interests of others before her own).

2. Flexibility

Here the person is flexible in her thinking, open to change, free from bigotry and pluralistic in her view of other people. She does not make rigid, invariant rules for herself and others.

3. Acceptance of uncertainty

Here the person fully accepts that we live in a world of probability and chance where absolute certainties do not and probably will never exist.

4. Commitment to vital absorbing interests

Here the person is likely to be healthier and happier when she is vitally absorbed in something outside herself than when she is not. This interest should be large enough to be involving and allow the person to express her talents and capacities.

5. Long-range hedonism

Here the person tends to seek a healthy balance between the pleasures of the moment and those of the future. She is prepared to put up with present pain if doing so is in her best interests and is likely to lead to future gain.

Figure 2.1. Examples of mental health criteria from an REBT perspective.

Module 3
Eliciting Commitment to Change

Introduction

It is not sufficient to elicit your client's goals. It is also important to elicit his commitment to change and work towards these goals. Therefore, in this module, I will discuss a method which you can use which is helpful in eliciting client commitment to change.

For your client to commit himself to change, it is important for him to see clearly that it is in his best interests to make the change. If your client does not see this, then he is hardly likely to commit himself to work towards his stated goal. You might ask, then, why your client might come up with a goal to which he is not committed. There may be a number of reasons for this. First, your client might identify a goal which others want him to achieve, but which he is either opposed to or ambivalent about. Thus, your client's parents may want him, for example, to become independent whereas he may wish to stay dependent or be in two minds about becoming independent. In order to help your client to commit himself to a goal, it is important to help him first evaluate fully the advantages and disadvantages of both the problem state and the alternative goal state. Over the years I have experimented with a number of ways of doing this. Having made several modifications to my approach of helping clients to weigh up the pros and cons of change, I now use a method which is quite comprehensive. I have devised a form called 'Cost–benefit analysis' which I encourage clients to complete, especially when it is clear that the client is ambivalent about change.

Unit 12: The cost–benefit analysis form: general principles

The cost–benefit analysis form which appears in Figure 3.1 is easy to complete and is based on a number of principles.

COST–BENEFIT ANALYSIS
ADVANTAGES/BENEFITS OF
Option 1

SHORT TERM

For yourself	For other people
1:.....................	1:.....................
2:.....................	2:.....................
3:.....................	3:.....................
4:.....................	4:.....................
5:.....................	5:.....................
6:.....................	6: ....

LONG TERM

For yourself	For other people
1:.....................	1:.....................
2:.....................	2:.....................
3:.....................	3:.....................
4:.....................	4:.....................
5:.....................	5:.....................
6:.....................	6:.....................

COST–BENEFIT ANALYSIS
ADVANTAGES/BENEFITS OF
Option 2

SHORT TERM

For yourself	For other people
1:.....................	1:.....................
2:.....................	2:.....................
3:.....................	3:.....................
4:.....................	4:.....................
5:.....................	5:.....................
6:.....................	6:.....................

LONG TERM

For yourself	For other people
1:.....................	1:.....................
2:.....................	2:.....................
3:.....................	3:.....................
4:.....................	4:.....................
5:.....................	5:.....................
6:.....................	6:.....................

DISADVANTAGES/COSTS OF
Option 1

SHORT TERM

For yourself	For other people
1:.....................	1:.....................
2:.....................	2:.....................
3:.....................	3:.....................
4:.....................	4:.....................
5:.....................	5:.....................
6:.....................	6:.....................

LONG TERM

For yourself	For other people
1:.....................	1:.....................
2:.....................	2:.....................
3:.....................	3:.....................
4:.....................	4:.....................
5:.....................	5:.....................
6:.....................	6:.....................

DISADVANTAGES/COSTS OF
Option 2

SHORT TERM

For yourself	For other people
1:.....................	1:.....................
2:.....................	2:.....................
3:.....................	3:.....................
4:.....................	4:.....................
5:.....................	5:.....................
6:.....................	6:.....................

LONG TERM

For yourself	For other people
1:.....................	1:.....................
2:.....................	2:.....................
3:.....................	3:.....................
4:.....................	4:.....................
5:.....................	5:.....................
6:.....................	6:.....................

Figure 3.1. The cost–benefit analysis form.

1. There is an alternative to the client's problem and it is important for you to help the client to put this in his own words.
2. The problem and the goal both have actual and perceived advantages and disadvantages.
3. These advantages and disadvantages operate both in the short term and in the long term.
4. These advantages and disadvantages are relevant for both your client and others in his life. This relevance is at its most obvious when your client's problem is interpersonal in nature; however, even when the problem does not seem to involve anybody else, it is still worthwhile asking your client to consider the advantages and disadvantages for himself and for others.

It is important to ask your client to complete the cost–benefit analysis form when he is in an objective frame of mind. Otherwise, you will receive an analysis heavily influenced by his psychologically disturbed state. This can best be done as a homework assignment because the form takes quite a while to complete and for you to do it with him in the session is not a cost-effective use of therapeutic time. Once your client has completed the form, ask him to put it away until the next therapy session. Otherwise, he may ruminate on it in an unproductive way.

When you go over the form with your client, first ask him to state what he learned from doing the task. If he states clearly that the goal is more attractive than the problem, you can ask him to commit himself formally to the goal. This may involve him making a written commitment which you could both sign. It could also involve him making a public declaration of some kind indicating his commitment to achieving the goal. Whilst making one or both types of formal commitment is not a necessary part of the REBT change process, these procedures do bring it home to the client that change is a serious business and one that is not to be entered into lightly.

You will note that I do not advocate going over the cost–benefit analysis form in detail with your client when he has stated that his goal is more desirable than the problem state and that he does wish to commit himself to achieving it. However, if you study the form carefully you will frequently gain a lot of information, especially from the 'advantages of the problem' section and the 'disadvantages of the goal' section concerning likely obstacles to client progress. Therefore, it is important that you retain a copy of the client's form and that you have it to hand when you are seeing him. It is also helpful if you encourage your client to keep a copy of the form to hand whenever he comes to therapy and at other times. Later, you will want to ask him to consult it for clues concerning obstacles to his continued progress.

When your client has completed the cost–benefit analysis form and is ambivalent about change or opts for the problem state over the goal state, then you need to go over the form with him in great detail. The purpose of doing this is to discover and deal with so-called advantages of the problem and perceived disadvantages of achieving the goal (I am assuming here that the goal is a healthy one, at least when taken at face value). Unless you deal with these sections of the form and correct the misconceptions you find there, it is not in the interests of either yourself or your client to ask him to commit himself to the goal. To do so under such circumstances is to get the change process off on the wrong foot. The following is an example of how to deal with such a situation. I will first present the client's cost–benefit analysis form (see Figure 3.2), then I will demonstrate how to challenge a client's misconceptions about the 'advantages' of the problem and the 'disadvantages' of achieving the goal. I will call the client in this example Sandra.

As you can see from Figure 3.2, Sandra is ambivalent about giving up 'sulking' (which is her general problem) and opting for the alternative 'communicating my feelings honestly to other people' which is Sandra's stated goal with respect to the general problem of sulking. Whilst you will most often use the cost–benefit analysis method with your client's general problems and goals, you can also use it with specific examples of general problems and related goals.

Unit 13: Responding to your client's perceived advantages of the problem and perceived disadvantages of achieving the goal

As Sandra is ambivalent about change it is important that I, as her therapist, review the form with her and respond in particular to the advantages she sees accompanying 'sulking' (her problem) and to the disadvantages that she sees accompanying 'communicating my feelings honestly to other people' (her stated goal). In Figure 3.3 I outline a summary of the specific arguments I used with Sandra as I challenged the misconceptions on which these 'advantages' and 'disadvantages' appeared to be based. As I will demonstrate later in the chapter, the way I helped Sandra to question her reasoning on this issue was by asking Socratic-type questions. The summary nature of the arguments presented in Figure 3.3 makes it appear that I just told Sandra why she was in error. As you will soon see, this was far from the case.

Unit 14: Using Socratic questions to help your client rethink the perceived advantages of the problem and the perceived disadvantages of the stated goal

You will note that many of the arguments that I used with Sandra are directed at her distorted inferences. Thus, taking the short-term advantage of sulking providing a good way of showing dissatisfaction, I show

Sandra that whilst this may be so, there are better ways of doing so. I also show her that sulking may lead to greater problems that she has not considered. Once again, it is very important for you to realise that the arguments presented in Figure 3.3 are summaries. That is why they appear in didactic form. In actuality, I engaged Sandra in a Socratic dialogue on the issue as the following interchange shows.

COST–BENEFIT ANALYSIS
ADVANTAGES/BENEFITS OF SULKING

SHORT TERM

For yourself	For other people
1. 'Safety valve' for anger	1. Lets people know I'm angry
2. Gives me time to think	2. Draws people's attention to a problem or mood
3. Release of frustration behaviour	3. Can jolt people into realising that their does have a negative effect
4. Shows dissatisfaction	4.
5. It's a sign of annoyance	5.
6.	6.

LONG TERM

For yourself	For other people
1. None	1. None
2.	2.
3.	3.
4.	4.
5.	5.
6.	6.

DISADVANTAGES/COSTS OF SULKING

SHORT TERM

For yourself	For other people
1. It's a waste of energy	1. It causes an uncomfortable atmosphere
2. It's debilitating	2. It creates tension in my relationship
3. It hides the real problem	3.
4.	4.
5.	5.
6.	6.

LONG TERM

For yourself	For other people
1. It puts me in a bad light with others	1. It causes a lot of misunderstandings
2.	2.
3.	3.
4.	4.
5.	5.
6.	6.

Figure 3.2. Sandra's cost–benefit analysis form.

COST–BENEFIT ANALYSIS
ADVANTAGES/BENEFITS OF COMMUNICATING MY FEELINGS HONESTLY TO OTHER PEOPLE

SHORT TERM

For yourself	For other people
1. Brings problems to a head	1. Brings problems to a head
2. Releases pent-up anger	2. Clarifies matters
3. May help to resolve matters	3. May help to resolve matters
4.	4.
5.	5.
6.	6.

LONG TERM

For yourself	For other people
1. Shows a determination to resolve matters	1. Allows for compromise
2. Represents more mature and positive action	2.
3.	3.
4.	4.
5.	5.
6.	6.

DISADVANTAGES/COSTS OF COMMUNICATING MY FEELINGS HONESTLY TO OTHER PEOPLE
SHORT TERM

For yourself	For other people
1. May say things I may regret	1. Heightens excitability and emotion–alism
2. I may lose relationships	2. They may feel hurt
3.	3.
4.	4.
5.	5.
6.	6.

LONG TERM

For yourself	For other people
1. May become unpopular	1. They may become wary of me
2. I may lose relationships	2. They may decide I'm too unpleasant to be around
3.	3.
4.	4.
5.	5.
6.	6.

Figure 3.2. Continued.

Windy: OK, Sandra. Now you say that a short-term advantage of sulking is that it helps you to show dissatisfaction. Do you see any way of showing dissatisfaction without sulking?

Sandra: Well, letting people know honestly that I am dissatisfied will have the same effect.

SHORT-TERM ADVANTAGES/BENEFITS OF SULKING

For yourself

1. 'Safety valve' for anger.

2. Gives me time to think.

3. Release of frustration.

4. Shows dissatisfaction.

5. It's a sign of annoyance.

Windy's response

1. Controlled honest communication is a more effective way of channelling anger. It is even more effective if you first challenge your anger-creating irrational beliefs and replace them with rational beliefs leading to healthy annoyance (see Dryden, 1995).

2. You don't need to sulk to give you time to think. There is a difference between withdrawing for yourself in order to give yourself time to think and withdrawal 'against the other' which is what sulking is. In fact, the latter detracts from the quality of your thinking while the former promotes this.

3. When you communicate honestly, you can release frustration, but in a way which is more likely to resolve problems than sulking.

4. While you do show dissatisfaction when you sulk you also show other things too, which are more likely to cause problems than solve them. When you communicate honestly you show dissatisfaction but again in a more constructive way than sulking.

5. The above argument is also relevant here. Honest communication is a more reliable and healthy way of communicating annoyance than sulking. In keeping the channel of communication open you are more likely to resolve matters by talking them through than with sulking which closes down the channel.

For other people

1. Lets them know I'm angry

2. Draws people's attention to a problem or mood.

Windy's response

1. Sulking may well let others know that you are angry, but it won't let them know what you're angry about. It is therefore liable to create more problems in this respect than it will solve.

2. Again sulking draws their attention to the fact that you have a problem, but it won't pinpoint the nature of the problem. By communicating honestly and openly you will let other people know exactly what your problem is.

Figure 3.3. Responding to Sandra's misconceptions about the 'advantages' of her problem and the 'disadvantages' of her stated goal.

3. Can jolt people into realising that their behaviour does have a negative effect.	3. This may happen, but what is more likely to happen is that you will jolt them into realising that your behaviour has a negative effect on them!

LONG-TERM ADVANTAGES/BENEFITS OF SULKING
None stated

SHORT-TERM DISADVANTAGES/COSTS OF COMMUNICATING MY FEELINGS HONESTLY TO OTHER PEOPLE

For yourself   *Windy's response*

1. May say things I may regret.	1. You are more likely to say things you may regret later when you are angry. That is why I recommend that you change the irrational beliefs that underpin your anger to rational beliefs that will enable you to be annoyed rather than angry. Annoyance is directed at the other's behaviour, while anger is directed at and puts down the other person.
2. I may lose relationships.	2. You are more likely to lose relationships if you sulk angrily than if you honestly convey your annoyance in a firm, but caring manner.

For other people

1. Heightens excitability and emotionalism.	1. If this is a disadvantage for other people, then honest communication of annoyance will reduce the intensity of the emotional atmosphere whereas honest communication of anger will increase excitability and emotionalism. That is another reason why I recommend that you first identify and challenge the irrational beliefs that underpin your anger and replace it with a set of rational beliefs that will allow you to communicate honestly and firmly, but caringly your feelings of annoyance.
2. They may feel hurt.	2. Yes, they may feel hurt when you honestly convey your annoyance even if you choose your words carefully. However, they are less likely to feel hurt when you communicate your feelings of annoyance than if you communicate your angry feelings. Also, don't forget that other people may feel hurt when you sulk. There is no way of guaranteeing that others won't be hurt no matter what you do. The more important consideration is whether you want your relationships with others to be based on honest communication or uncommunicative sulking.

Figure 3.3. Continued.

LONG-TERM DISADVANTAGES/COSTS OF COMMUNICATING MY FEELINGS HON-
ESTLY TO OTHER PEOPLE

For yourself   *Windy's response*

1. May become unpopular   1. Yes, you may become unpopular if you
                                        honestly communicate your feelings of
                                        annoyance. However, I would argue that in
                                        the long term you will be even more
                                        unpopular if you sulk or communicate your
                                        anger. Don't forget either that honest
                                        communication also involves expression of
                                        positive feelings. If you are open about your
                                        good feelings about others as well as your
                                        negative feelings about them then you will in
                                        all probability increase your popularity.

2. May lose relationships.   2. Again you may lose relationships if you
                                        communicate honestly, but if you
                                        communicate feelings of annoyance you will
                                        lose less relationships in the long-term than if
                                        you sulk or honestly communicate your
                                        other-damning angry feelings. This will
                                        especially be the case if you also
                                        communicate your positive feelings to other
                                        people.

For other people

1. They may become wary of me.   1. This is true, but they will probably become
                                        equally wary of you when they discover that
                                        you sulk. Also expressions of anger are more
                                        likely to lead to others being wary of you
                                        than expressions of healthy annoyance.

2. They may decide I'm too   2. This seems to be more a disadvantage for
   unpleasant to be around.   you than for others. Even if it is a disadvan-
                                        tage for them, I would argue, as I have done
                                        before, that this is more likely to happen if
                                        you sulk or show your anger than if you show
                                        your annoyance.

Figure 3.3. Continued.

Windy: Right. Incidentally, if you sulk how do you know that in people's minds you are not showing other things too, like anger or puni-
tiveness?

Sandra: I guess I don't.

Windy: So which is a more reliable guide to showing dissatisfaction:
sulking or honestly communicating your feelings?

Sandra: Honest communication.

Windy: Does that change your view that a short-term advantage of sulking is that it helps you to show dissatisfaction?

Sandra: Yes. It helps me to see that sulking shows a number of things other than dissatisfaction and these other things like anger won't be beneficial to my relationships.

Unit 15: Reconsidering the cost–benefit analysis and asking for a commitment to change

After you have helped your client to review the 'advantages' of his or her problem and the 'disadvantages' of the stated goal, it is important that you encourage him or her to reconsider his cost–benefit analysis of the problem and the goal. You can do this in two ways. First, you can have the client take his or her old cost–benefit analysis form and write in a different colour pen the reasons why the problem's perceived advantages are, in fact, not benefits and the reasons why the goal's perceived disadvantages are not, in fact, costs. Second, you can ask your client to complete a second cost–benefit analysis form which, if you have been successful in helping to correct the previous misconceptions, should demonstrate a clear preference for his or her stated goal. If not, you need to proceed as above until a clear preference for one of the two options is demonstrated.

Concerning eliciting a commitment to change let me quote the point I made on this issue on page 67, as it is worth reiterating: 'If he or she (i.e. your client) states clearly that the goal is more attractive than the problem, you can ask for a formal commitment to the goal. This may involve him or her making a written commitment which you could both sign. It could also involve him or her making a public declaration of some kind indicating commitment to achieving the goal. Whilst making one or both types of formal commitment is not a necessary part of the REBT change process, these procedures do bring it home to the client that change is a serious business and one that is not to be entered into lightly.'

You will find, in conclusion, that the disputing process (which is the subject of the following module) will go more smoothly when your client has made a commitment to his stated goal than when he is still ambivalent about change. Trying to dispute your client's irrational beliefs without eliciting such a commitment is like running a race with a ball and chain around one leg. Encouraging your client to make this commitment is the key which removes such an impediment.

Module 4
Disputing Irrational
Beliefs: An Introduction

In the following modules on disputing, I will deal with one of the core skills you will need as an REBT therapist — disputing your client's irrational beliefs. In order to help you do this successfully, I will discuss five topics. First, because you need to ensure that you have prepared your client for the disputing process I will begin by considering this issue in this module. Second, I will cover the three major arguments you will need to use in helping your client to question the rationality of her irrational beliefs (Module 5). Third, I will describe the two major disputing styles you will need to master if you are to vary your approach with different clients (Modules 6 and 7) and discuss flexibility in disputing (Module 8). Fourth, I will illustrate some of this material by presenting and commenting on a transcript of Albert Ellis disputing the irrational beliefs of one of his clients (Module 9). Finally, in Module 10, I will show you how you can help your client to bring to the fore her rational beliefs.

Unit 16: Preparing your client for the disputing process

What are the preparatory steps that you need to take before you dispute your client's irrational beliefs? I have covered most of these issues in the first volume in this series (Dryden, 1995), and in the earlier modules of this book. Consequently I will only summarise the points here.

Teach the effect of irrational beliefs on psychological disturbance

If you are to engage your client in the disputing process, then you need to help her to understand the central role that irrational beliefs play in the development and maintenance of psychological problems in general (see Dryden, 1995).

Assess the client's target problem

If your client is get the most out of the disputing process, then you need to help her to see the role that her specific irrational beliefs play in the development and maintenance of her specific target problem. You can best do this by carrying out an accurate ABC assessment of this target problem. It is particularly important that your client underscores its accuracy. If she does not do this, re-assess her target problem until she does so (see Dryden, 1995).

Identify your client's goal and elicit commitment to change

Ed Bordin (1979) has made a useful distinction between the goals and tasks of psychotherapy. He notes that the purpose of therapeutic tasks is to help clients achieve their therapeutic goals. According to Bordin, then, disputing your client's irrational beliefs is a therapeutic task, the object of which is to help your client achieve her goal. Consequently, as discussed in Modules 2 and 3, helping your client to identify and commit herself to her stated goal for change is an important prerequisite for disputing her irrational beliefs. Unless this is done the disputing process will tend to be directionless.

Helping your client to see the relevance of disputing her irrational beliefs as a primary means of achieving her goal

As well as helping your client to see that her irrational beliefs underpin her target problem, it is equally important that you help her to see that changing these beliefs will help her to achieve her stated goal with respect to this problem. Here is an example of how to do this.

Windy: So, recapping on the ABC of your anxiety, C is your feelings of anxiety, A is the event in your mind that your boss will disapprove of you and B is your irrational belief: 'My boss must not disapprove of me. I am less worthy if he does.' Is that accurate?

Victor: Yes it is.

Windy: From this assessment can you see what largely determines your feelings of anxiety?

Victor: The belief that my boss must not disapprove of me.

Windy: Now let's recap on your goal. What would be a more healthy, but realistic response to receiving disapproval from your boss than anxiety?

Victor: As we said before, to feel concerned but not anxious about it.

Windy: So if your belief that your boss must not disapprove of you leads to your anxiety and your goal is to feel concerned, but not anxious about this possibility, what do we have to help you to change in order for you to achieve your goal?

Victor: We have to change my belief.

Helping your client to understand what disputing involves

As I will discuss in greater detail in Module 6, disputing involves you asking your client a number of questions designed to encourage her to evaluate the rationality of her irrational beliefs and explaining any points about which she is not clear. As such it is useful to help your client understand what you will be doing and why you will be doing it. An example follows from my work with Victor.

Windy: Right, you need to change your irrational belief. The way I can best help you to do this is to encourage you to see why your irrational belief is, in fact, irrational. I will be doing this by asking you a number of questions designed to help you to understand this point. The reason why I will be asking you questions in the first instance is to help you to think about this issue for yourself. This is what Socrates, a famous Greek philosopher, did with his students. He didn't tell them the answers to various difficult philosophical questions. Rather, he asked them a series of questions, the purpose of which was to help them discover the answers for themselves. He helped them with his questions to be sure, but he didn't do the work for them. However, if my questioning doesn't help you to understand any given point I will provide you with an explanation which will I hope clarifies the point. I won't, in other words, leave you up in the air. Does what I say make sense to you?

Victor: Yes. What you're saying is that you will help me to re-evaluate my irrational belief by asking me questions about it. And you'll explain any points that I don't understand.

Windy: Shall we start?

Victor: Go ahead.

Module 5
Disputing Irrational Beliefs: The Three Major Arguments

The noted American REBT therapist, Ray DiGiuseppe, and his trainees listened to numerous audiotapes of Albert Ellis conducting therapy in order to understand better the disputing process (DiGiuseppe, 1991). As part of their analysis, DiGiuseppe and his trainees discovered that Ellis employed three major arguments while disputing his clients' irrational beliefs.

Unit 17: What are the three major arguments?

The three arguments that Ellis used were as follows:

1. Empirical Arguments. Empirical arguments are designed to encourage your client to look for empirical evidence which confirms or disconfirms his or her irrational beliefs. The basic question here is this: are your irrational beliefs realistic or consistent with reality?
2. Logical Arguments. Logical arguments are designed to encourage your client to examine whether or not his or her irrational beliefs are logical. The basic question here is this: do your irrational beliefs follow logically from your rational beliefs?
3. Pragmatic Arguments. Pragmatic arguments are designed to encourage your client to question the utilitarian nature of his or her irrational beliefs. The basic question here is this: do your irrational beliefs help you or hinder you as you pursue your stated goals?

Now that I have described the three major arguments, I will outline the points you need to make as you apply these arguments while disputing the four irrational beliefs: musts; awfulising; low frustration tolerance and self/other downing. As I do so please note that my focus is on the content of the arguments not the way they are presented. I will deal with this latter point in Modules 6 and 7.

Unit 18: Using the three major arguments with musts

You will recall from the first volume in this series (Dryden, 1995), that musts are absolutistic evaluative beliefs which, according to REBT theory, are at the core of psychological disturbance. From these musts are derived three other irrational beliefs, i.e. awfulising, low frustration tolerance and self/other downing. Musts are irrational for the following reasons.

Empirical — musts are inconsistent with reality

Let's take Victor's irrational belief: 'My boss must not disapprove of me.' If there was a law of the universe which stated that Victor's boss must not disapprove of him, then it would be impossible for the boss to do so no matter what Victor did. Such a law of the universe would forbid Victor's boss from ever disapproving of him. As it is always possible for his boss to disapprove of Victor, this proves that there is no empirical evidence to support Victor's irrational belief that: 'My boss must not disapprove of me.'

If Victor's irrational belief were true it would mean that Victor's boss would lack free will. He would be deprived of his human right to form a negative opinion of Victor. As the boss does have the freedom to think negatively of Victor, this fact empirically disconfirms Victor's irrational belief.

If Victor's boss did ever disapprove of him, this would contradict Victor's belief. If, under these circumstances, Victor still believed that his boss absolutely should not have disapproved of him, then this would be tantamount to Victor believing: 'what just happened absolutely should not have happened', or 'reality must not be reality' which empirically is nonsense.

Logical — musts do not follow logically from preferences

Victor has a healthy rational belief which is stated in the form of a preference: 'I would prefer it if my boss did not disapprove of me.' However, his irrational belief: 'My boss must not disapprove of me' does not follow logically from his preferential rational belief. Rigid musts and non-dogmatic preferences are not in any way logically connected. So if Victor were to state rationally that it would be preferable if his boss did not disapprove of him and conclude that as a result his boss must not disapprove of him, then his conclusion: 'my boss must not disapprove of me' would not be logically related to his rational belief: 'It would be preferable if my boss did not disapprove of me.' In short it would be an illogical conclusion.

Pragmatic — musts lead to poor psychological results

Victor's irrational demand that his boss must not disapprove of him is likely to lead to poor emotional, cognitive and behavioural results. Thus, if Victor holds this belief in a situation where his boss approves of him, but there is a slight chance that he may incur such disapproval, then he will tend to get anxious and will tend to think and act in certain ways associated with anxiety (see Dryden, 1995, Figure 5.1). In addition, if Victor receives clear evidence that his boss does disapprove of him, then his 'must' will lead him to feel anxiety, depression or anger and again he will tend to think and act in self-defeating ways that relate to whichever unhealthy negative emotion predominates (see Dryden, 1995, Figure 5.1).

Victor's irrational demand that his boss must not disapprove of him will interfere with his stated goal. For example, if he wants to be healthily concerned about the prospect of being disapproved of by his boss, but not anxious about him, then his must will constitute a major obstacle to Victor achieving this goal.

Unit 19: Using the three major arguments with awfulising

According to REBT theory, awfulising is an irrational derivative of a primary must. It represents the tendency to evaluate events in grossly exaggerated, dogmatic ways. Awfulising is irrational for the following reasons.

Empirical – 'nothing is awful in the universe'

Ellis defines the term 'awful' when used in its absolute disturbance-creating sense as more than 100% bad, worse than it absolutely must be. As such, because you can never reach awful, it empirically does not exist. As I have already noted, Smokey Robinson's mother's advice to her son aptly illustrates this idea: 'From the day you are born, 'til you ride in the hearse, there's nothing so bad that it couldn't be worse.' Thus, awfulising is not a property of the natural world; rather, it is a concept that constitutes a creation of the human mind.

Consequently, when Victor concludes: 'It would be awful if my boss disapproved of me', he is making an empirically unsupportable statement because he can presumably think of many occurrences that would be worse than being disapproved of by his boss.

Logical – awfulising represents an illogical over-generalisation from non-dogmatic ratings of badness

It would be healthy for Victor to conclude that it would be bad if his boss disapproved of him. However, if he were to conclude that it would be awful if his boss disapproved of him, his awfulising belief would not follow logically from his healthy evaluation of badness. Evaluations of badness lie on a continuum from 0–99.9% badness, whereas awfulising lies on a magical continuum from 101%–infinity. As you can see there is no logical connection between the two continua.

Pragmatic – awfulising leads to poor psychological results

Victor's irrational belief that it would be awful if his boss disapproved of him is likely to lead to poor emotional, cognitive and behavioural results. Thus, if Victor holds this belief in a situation where his boss approves of him, but there is a slight chance that he may incur such disapproval, then he will again tend to get anxious and to think and act in ways associated with anxiety (see Dryden, 1995, Figure 5.1). In addition, if Victor receives clear evidence that his boss does disapprove of him, then his awfulising belief will lead him to feel anxiety, depression or anger and again he will tend to think and act in self-defeating ways that relate to whichever unhealthy negative emotion predominates (see Dryden, 1995, Figure 5.1).

Victor's belief that it would be awful if his boss disapproved of him will interfere with his stated goal. Thus, if he wants to be healthily concerned about the prospect of being disapproved of by his boss, but not anxious about him, then his awfulising will constitute a major obstacle to Victor achieving this goal because it will lead to anxiety and not concern.

Unit 20: Using the three major arguments with low frustration tolerance

According to REBT theory, low frustration tolerance is another irrational derivative of a primary must. It represents the position that one cannot tolerate frustrating or uncomfortable situations. This belief is irrational for the following reasons.

Empirical — you can bear the so-called unbearable

If it were true that you couldn't tolerate a frustrating or uncomfortable situation then you would literally die or you would never experience any happiness for the rest of your life, no matter how you thought about the situation in question. Thus, if it were true that Victor couldn't tolerate being disapproved of by his boss, as he believes, then if this disapproval occurred Victor would have to die or forfeit any chance of future happiness. Obviously, neither of these two things would happen. The ironic thing about a philosophy of low frustration tolerance is that even when Victor tells himself that he can't stand his boss's disapproval he is standing it. Now he could tolerate it better and you can help him to do so. But the point is that he is tolerating it even when he is doing so poorly. Thus, it is completely anti-empirical to believe that you can't stand something even when it is very difficult to bear.

In this context, I ask clients who believe they cannot stand something whether they could stand it if it meant saving the life of a loved one. They invariably say 'yes'. This proves that the 'I can't stand it' statement is again anti-empirical because, if it were true that they couldn't stand the relevant situation, they would not be able to stand it under any circumstances.

Logical — it makes no logical sense to conclude that you can't stand something because it is difficult to tolerate

Once again it is healthy for Victor to believe that it would be difficult for him to tolerate his boss's disapproval. However, it would be illogical for him to conclude that because this would be hard to bear, it would therefore be unbearable. If something is difficult to bear, it is still bearable; thus Victor's conclusion is really this: because I am tolerating my boss's disapproval, it is therefore intolerable. This is clearly illogical nonsense.

Pragmatic — low frustration tolerance leads to poor psychological results

The points that I made with respect to the pragmatic consequences of holding musts and awfulising beliefs are also relevant to low frustration tolerance beliefs. Victor's irrational belief that he could not stand it if his boss disapproved of him is likely to lead to poor emotional, cognitive and behavioural results. Thus, again if Victor holds this belief in a situation where his boss approves of him, but there is a slight chance that he may incur such disapproval, then he will tend to get anxious and to think and act in ways associated with anxiety (see Dryden, 1995, Figure 5.1). In addition, if Victor receives clear evidence that his boss does disapprove of him, then his LFT belief will lead him to feel anxiety, depression or anger and again he will tend to think and act in self-defeating ways that relate to whichever unhealthy negative emotion predominates (see Dryden, 1995, Figure 5.1).

Furthermore, Victor's belief that he could not stand it if his boss disapproved of him will interfere with his stated goal. Thus, if he wants to be healthily concerned about the prospect of being disapproved of by his boss, but not anxious about this, then his LFT belief will constitute a major obstacle to Victor achieving this goal because it will lead to anxiety and not concern.

Unit 21: Using the three major arguments with self/other downing

According to REBT theory, self/other downing is yet another irrational derivative of a primary must. It represents the position that the worth or value of a person varies according to changing conditions. The common factor linking self-downing and other-downing is the philosophy of downing. As such, I will concentrate my discussion on self-downing. However, similar points could be made for the concept of other-downing. Self-downing is irrational for the following reasons.

Empirical — it is empirically untenable to rate the 'self'

Self-downing is known in common parlance as low self-esteem (LSE). Most clients with LSE wish to have HSE (high self-esteem). However, both rest on the idea that it is possible to rate (i.e. esteem) the 'self'. Is this in fact possible? To answer this question we need to define what we mean by the 'self'. Paul Hauck's (1991) definition of the self is as good as any (and better than most) so I will use it to construct my argument that it is empirically untenable to rate the 'self'. Hauck (1991), then, defines the 'self' as 'every conceivable thing about you that can be rated' (p. 33). As such, your 'self' is too complex to be given a single rating. Such an evaluation would be possible if you were a single-cell amoeba; but you are a human organism who has millions of thoughts and feelings, has acted in countless ways and has very many traits and characteristics. Consequently, you cannot give your 'self' a legitimate rating. You can and probably do give your 'self' an illegitimate rating, but this evaluation has nothing to do with the reality of who you are.

Even if it were possible to give your 'self' a single rating with the help of a computer so powerful that it hasn't been invented yet, such an evaluation would be out of date as soon as it was made. Why? Because you are not static, but constantly in flux. A rating, once made, is a static thing and thus cannot do justice to an ongoing, ever-changing organism.

Thus if Victor concluded that he was a bad person if his boss disapproved of him then he would be making an unempirical statement. If it were true that Victor were a bad person then everything about him would have to be bad now, in the past and in the future. This is hardly likely.

Logical — whilst you can legitimately rate single aspects of your 'self', it does not follow logically that you can rate your whole 'self'.

It makes logical sense to rate given aspects of your 'self' because doing so helps you to determine whether or not these aspects aid you in the pursuit of your basic goals and purposes. Having rated a given aspect, however, it is illogical then to proceed to rate your entire 'self'. Doing so involves making the logical error of over-generalisation or what is known as the part–whole error. Here you assign a rating to your entire self on the basis of your evaluation of a part of your self. Another name for this illogicality is prejudice.

Thus, if Victor concluded that he was a bad person if his boss disapproved of him then he would be making an illogical statement. He would take a negative situation (i.e. his boss's situation) and conclude on the basis of this that his whole 'self' was bad — a clear over-generalisation.

Pragmatic — self-downing leads to poor psychological results

Victor's irrational self-downing in the face of his boss's disapproval is likely to lead to poor emotional, cognitive and behavioural results before the fact of the disapproval and after that fact. The same points that I made about the pragmatic consequences of musts, awfulising and LFT beliefs also apply to self-downing beliefs.

I made the point earlier that rating a specific aspect of yourself is useful in that doing so helps you to determine whether or not this aspect aids you in your pursuit towards your long-term goals and, thus, whether you need to change it. However, rating your 'self' over and above the rating you assign to that given aspect does not give you added benefit as you strive to determine whether or not the aspect is goal-enhancing. Indeed, rating your 'self' will hamper you in your deliberations about the usefulness of the specific aspect of yourself. In this situation, while you are trying to think about the usefulness of the specific aspect, you simultaneously give your 'self' a single (often negative) rating. Trying to do two things at once will interfere with your major task — judging the utilitarian value of the aspect under consideration.

Unit 22: The importance of order in disputing

Before completing this module, I want to stress one important point. When you dispute your client's irrational belief it is best for you to do so one at a time and to use one argument at a time. Otherwise, you will 'bounce around' from one belief to the next and from one argument to the next. Let's suppose that you have chosen to target your client's must for change and to employ an empirical argument first. As this is your chosen strategy persist with it until your client has grasped the point or shows signs that he or she is unlikely to understand that there is no empirical evidence for the existence of a must. In which case, switch to employing, say, a logical argument to dispute the same must.

Persist with this tack until your client has again understood the illogical nature of his or her 'must' or is unlikely to grasp your meaning. Then, switch to using the remaining argument (in this case, the pragmatic one) until one of the two criteria for stopping disputing has been met. Then use the same three arguments, one at a time, with one or more of the client's irrational belief derivatives of her primary must.

Figure 5.1 shows a good sequence of disputing as demonstrated in the work of Therapist A. Here the first twenty responses made by Therapist A were analysed response by response by looking at which type of irrational belief was targeted for change and which of the three major arguments was employed. Then the first twenty responses of Therapist B were analysed in the same way. This therapist's work shows a poor sequence of disputing. Of course a therapist's responses will be influenced by the client's prior response and it is likely that Therapist B had to deal with a client who was less ordered. However, it is your responsibility as an REBT therapist to help to structure your client's thinking rather than follow his chaos as Therapist B did. In clinical practice it is impossible to achieve perfect sequencing on a consistent

Therapist A			Therapist B		
Response	Belief	Argument	Response	Belief	Argument
1	Must	Empirical	1	Must	Empirical
2	Must	Empirical	2	Must	Pragmatic
3	Must	Empirical	3	Awfulising	Pragmatic
4	Must	Empirical	4	LFT	Logical
5	Must	Pragmatic	5	LFT	Logical
6	Must	Pragmatic	6	Must	Logical
7	Must	Logical	7	LFT	Empirical
8	Must	Logical	8	LFT	Pragmatic
9	Must	Logical	9	Awfulising	Empirical
10	Must	Logical	10	Must	Empirical
11	Must	Logical	11	Awfulising	Logical
12	Must	Logical	12	Must	Logical
13	LFT	Empirical	13	Must	Logical
14	LFT	Empirical	14	Must	Empirical
15	LFT	Pragmatic	15	LFT	Empirical
16	LFT	Pragmatic	16	Awfulising	Empirical
17	LFT	Logical	17	Awfulising	Logical
18	LFT	Logical	18	LFT	Logical
19	LFT	Logical	19	LFT	Empirical
20	LFT	Logical	20	Must	Empirical

Figure 5.1. Analysis of two therapists' disputing responses by belief target and argument employed.

basis, so don't become perfectionistic on this issue. One way to discover how much order you are bringing to your disputing work with clients is to tape record your sessions and apply the same analysis on your disputing work that I have demonstrated in Figure 5.1. As long as there is a discernible degree of order in your work, you are probably doing well enough. If there is the chaos characteristic of the work of Therapist B, then seek help from your REBT supervisor and/or trainer.

Having considered the three main arguments you can use while disputing your client's irrational beliefs and having applied these arguments to the four main irrational beliefs, I will now move on to consider the two major styles of disputing. As a beginning practitioner of rational emotive behaviour therapy, you need to develop competence in both major styles of disputing: Socratic and didactic. Clients will differ in the value they derive from these different styles, so you may need to make predominant use of Socratic disputing with one client and didactic disputing with another. You will discover, though, that you frequently need to use both with a given client. Whichever style of disputing you use the purpose of each style is the same — to help the client gain intellectual insight into the irrationality of his or her irrational beliefs and the rationality of his or her alternative rational beliefs, using the kind of arguments I discussed in the previous section.

Module 6
Socratic Disputing of Irrational Beliefs

As I briefly showed earlier, Socrates educated his students by asking them open-ended questions designed to encourage them to think critically about philosophical problems. He knew the answers to these problems, but he saw that there was little to be gained by telling his students the solutions. Rather, his goal was to help his pupils, through his questioning procedure, gain a way of thinking about philosophical problems which they could then apply to a broad range of questions and, most importantly, which they could use in his absence. This is similar to the sage who said that if you plant a crop for hungry people you help them now, but if you teach them how to plant crops you help them to help themselves now and in the future. Thus, when you employ Socratic-type questions while disputing your client's irrational beliefs, you are not only helping him or her to question the rationality of these beliefs in the present, but you are also helping him or her to develop a methodology for questioning the rationality of irrational beliefs in the future.

When you ask a Socratic-type question in disputing, it is important to take great care to evaluate your client's response. In particular, you need to monitor four likely responses: (i) the client has answered your question correctly; (ii) the client has answered your question incorrectly; (iii) the client has misunderstood your question and has provided an answer to a different question; (iv) the client has changed the subject.

Let me deal with each of these situations in turn.

Unit 23: Socratic disputing when your client has answered your question correctly

When your client has answered your question correctly, it is important to assess the status of her answer. Has she given you the correct answer because she thinks it is what you want to hear? If so, does she also see the sense of it or is she looking for your approval? You need to examine these issues and deal with them (Socratically if possible) until your client sees for herself the correctness of her answer and provides it for no other reason than that it is the correct answer.

For example:

Windy: So where is the evidence that you must pass your exams?

Fiona: There isn't any.

Windy: Why isn't there?

Fiona: Because if there was such a law I could not fail.

Windy: Do you believe that because you're convinced of it or because it is the answer you think I want to hear?

Fiona: ...(pause)...Well, to be frank because it's the answer I think you want to hear.

Windy: What if I wanted to hear the opposite answer?

Fiona: Well...I would still believe it.

Windy: Even if I was disappointed?

Fiona: Yes.

Windy: Why?

Fiona: Because it is true.

Windy: How would you defend it to a friend then?...

Unit 24: Socratic disputing when your client has answered your question incorrectly

When your client has answered your question incorrectly, you need to use her answer to formulate another Socratic question. Keep doing this until your client has understood the rational point. For example:

Windy: So where is the evidence that you must pass your exams?

Fiona: Well, if I don't I'll find it harder to get a job.

[Here the client has provided evidence why not passing her exams would have disadvantages for her. She has not, though, provided evidence in support of the idea that she must do so.]

Windy: Is finding it harder to get a job evidence for the idea that you must pass your exams or for the idea that it is undesirable if you fail?

Fiona: Put like that, it's evidence for it being undesirable.

Windy: Do you have any other evidence in support of your belief that you must pass your exams?

Fiona: Well, my parents will be very upset if I fail.

Windy: Again, is that evidence in support of the idea that it is undesirable if you fail or that you absolutely must pass?

Fiona: It's undesirable.

Windy: Any other evidence in support of the idea that you must pass?

Fiona: I guess not.

Windy: What do you conclude from that?

Fiona: That I want to pass my exams, but there is no law that states that I have to do so.

Unit 25: Socratic disputing when your client has misunderstood your question and answers a different question

What do you do when your client thinks you have asked her a different question? If this is the case bring this to her attention as Socratically as you can, although you probably cannot avoid making an explanatory statement during this process. For example:

Windy: So, where is the evidence that you must pass your exams?

Fiona: I know exams are not a good way of assessing people, but they do need to be taken you know.

[Here it is clear that the client is responding to a very different question.]

Windy: Did you think I asked you why you consider exams to be a good way of assessing people or where is the evidence that you must pass yours?

Fiona: Oh. Did I hear you wrongly? Let me see...Sorry, can you ask me the question again?

Windy: Where is the evidence that you absolutely must pass your exams?

Fiona: I guess there is none...

Unit 26: Socratic disputing when your client changes the subject

Finally, how do you respond when your client changes the subject? Here you have a number of options. First, you may consider that the client is following her train of thought rather than yours. In ordinary conversation, people do suddenly change the direction of a conversation because something the other person has said sparks off a thought in the person's mind which she then articulates. If you think this is the case, this is how you might respond:

Windy: So where is the evidence that you must pass your exams?

Fiona: You know my friend Jane is coming down this weekend.

Windy: Sorry, I'm a bit confused. Can you help me understand the connection between looking for evidence for the belief that you must pass your exams and your friend Jane visiting you this weekend?

Fiona: I'm sorry. You asking me that question reminded me that Jane's exams finish on Friday and she promised to come down as they were over.

Windy: So you are looking forward to seeing her. But do you think you will be able to concentrate on challenging your belief about having to pass your exams if we go back to it?

Fiona: I'm sure I will.

Windy: So where is the evidence that you must pass your exams?...

At other times you will recognise that your client's change of topic while you are disputing her irrational belief is probably related to other, less benign factors. First, your client may have difficulty in keeping her attention on what you are both discussing. In this instance, ask your client for permission to interrupt her when she deviates from the issue and bring her back to the disputing sequence. If this doesn't work and you notice that it happens frequently no matter what you are discussing, it is probably a good idea to refer your client for a neuropsychological assessment or in cases of more profound attentional impairment for a neurological examination.

Second, you may suspect that your client finds your Socratic questions threatening in some way and thus she deals with the threat by avoiding the issue. If this is the case, it may be that your client finds the content of your questions threatening. For example, Fiona may change the subject because she does not want to face up to the issue that she has a problem with her exams or she does not want to confront the fact that she may be thinking irrationally about this issue. If correct, these constitute evidence that the client may have a meta-emotional problem which warrants exploration and intervention. You may need to switch focus and do this if it is the case. Alternatively, your client may find the process of Socratic questioning difficult and she may change the subject to cope with her discomfort. If this is the case, you may wish to be more didactic or, if you deem it important, you may wish to encourage her to tolerate her feelings of discomfort and persist with the Socratic questioning. Here is an example of dealing with one of these scenarios:

Windy: So where is the evidence that you must pass your exams?

Fiona: You know my friend Jane is coming down this weekend.

Windy: Fiona, you seemed to change the subject again when I asked you for evidence for your belief. Is there anything that you find uncomfortable about the question?

Fiona: Well...your question reminds me that I'm not handling this situation well.

[This is a clue that the client may have a hitherto undiscovered meta-emotional problem.]

Windy: And as you focus on the fact, and let's assume for the moment that it is a fact, that you aren't handling the situation well, how do you feel about that?

Fiona: Ashamed.

Windy: Given that you feel ashamed every time I question you about your demand that you must pass you exams, does that explain why you change the subject?

Fiona: Yes it does.

Windy: So shall we stick with challenging your demand to pass your exam or shall we deal with your feelings of shame first?

Fiona: I think we need to deal with the shame first.

This example demonstrates something interesting. Even though you may have worked carefully in the assessment phase of therapy to identify a meta-emotional problem, it may only be at the disputing phase that you discover that one exists and that it interferes with the work you are doing on your client's primary target problem. Sometimes you will only learn of the presence of a meta-emotional problem when your client acts to avoid discussing issues that he finds personally threatening (see Dryden, 1994b).

Unit 27: Examples of Socratic questions

In module 9 I present disputing strategies carried out by Albert Ellis which illustrate the kind of Socratic questions that he asks. But, first, I will list some Socratic-type questions for each of the three major arguments discussed earlier; the target of the questions will be a must.

Empirical

* Where is the evidence that you must...?
* Is there any evidence that you must...?

* Where is the law of the universe which states that you must...?
* Is there a law of the universe which states that you must...?
* If there were a law of the universe which stated that you must, how do you account for the fact that you didn't do what the law dictated that you do?
* Would a scientist think that there was evidence in support of your must?

Logical

* Where is the logic that you must...?
* Is it logical to believe that you must...?
* Does it logically follow that because you want to...therefore you must...?
* Does that must logically follow from your preference?
* Is it good logic to believe that because you want...therefore you must...?
* Would a philosopher think that it was good logic to believe that because you want to...therefore you must...?

Pragmatic

* Where will it get you to believe that you must...?
* What are the emotional and behavioural consequences of believing that you must...?
* Will that must give you good results?
* Is it healthy for you to believe that you must...?
* How is believing that you must...going to help you achieve your (long-term/healthy) goals?
* Is believing that you must...going to help or hinder you in the pursuit of your (long-term/healthy) goals?

Module 7
Didactic Disputing of Irrational Beliefs

The term 'didactic disputing' is actually something of a misnomer because when you are being didactic in REBT you are teaching the client by telling him why irrational beliefs are irrational and why rational beliefs are rational. So the essence of didactic disputing is teaching rational principles by explanation, using the same three major arguments that have been reviewed earlier in this book, i.e. empirical, logical and pragmatic.

What I will do in this module is outline several criteria for good practice when disputing didactically. In doing so, I will also alert you to the most common problems that novice REBT therapists experience when using didactic disputing methods.

Unit 28: Keep your didactic explanations as short as possible

When you are challenging your client's irrational beliefs by providing her with information designed to cast doubt on the empirical, logical and pragmatic status of these beliefs, it is important that you keep your explanations as brief as possible. Otherwise you will provide your client with too much information to process adequately. Of course, clients will vary quite considerably with respect to how much information they can process at a given time and you will want to take this issue into account when deciding how much information to provide your client with. If you are in doubt here, err on the side of caution and provide your client with less information than you believe she can digest.

As a training exercise, tape record your therapy sessions and listen particularly to your didactic explanations. Write out ways in which you could have shortened your explanations and show these to your REBT trainer or supervisor. Also play them the relevant taped segment so that they can compare what you said to your client with the proposed shortened version.

Unit 29: Periodically check your client's level of understanding of the points you are didactically presenting to her

The purpose of presenting your client with information in a didactic manner is to help her to LEARN rational principles which she can later apply in her everyday life. I have emphasised the word LEARN here because many novice REBT therapists think that the goal of didactic disputing is to teach rather than to encourage the client to learn. As the emphasis here is on client learning rather than on therapist teaching, you need to ensure, in the first instance, that your client understands the points you are didactically presenting to her. You can best do this by periodically asking her questions like: 'I'm not sure that I'm making myself clear, can you put into your own words what you've heard me say?'

Note, in particular, two points about this question:

(i) It puts the burden on the therapist to make herself clear rather than on the client to understand.

(ii) It encourages the client to be an active rather than a passive learner by asking her to put her understanding of what you have said into her own words. If your client still uses the same words as you employed, gently encourage her to reformulate her understanding of your points in different language.

If in doing so your client makes errors of understanding, correct these prefacing your remarks by saying something like: 'I don't think that I phrased my explanation very well. Let me see if I can put it another way.'

This again shows that you are taking primary responsibility for your client understanding the rational message. If you don't do this your client may well blame herself for her failure to comprehend what you have been saying. Having prefaced your remarks in this way, make your point again and once more elicit your client's understanding. Proceed in this manner until your client has understood the point you have been making.

Unit 30: Once your client has understood a substantive rational point, ask her for her views on it

Just because your client has understood a rational point, it does not follow that she agrees with it. Thus, after your client has understood the substantive point you have been making, ask her for her views on it. Does she agree or disagree with it? Does she think that the point has some practical value for her? Don't be afraid to debate an issue with your client or to correct any misconceptions that she might reveal.

However, do so in a non-defensive way and without attacking your client in any way.

Module 8
Flexibility in Disputing

As you learn more about disputing, you will discover that it is a difficult skill that needs to be used flexibly. Whilst a full discussion of this point is beyond this book, I will give you an example of the flexible use of disputing. (For a fuller discussion of the complexity of disputing see DiGiuseppe, 1991.)

Unit 31: Using the two styles of disputing conjointly

Having introduced the two disputing styles, how are you to know which style to use with which client? Whilst this is a difficult and complex question to answer fully, let me give you this rule of thumb. Some clients will resonate to a predominantly Socratic style of disputing. These will basically be intelligent clients who are accustomed to thinking for themselves. For other clients who are less intelligent and are less used to reflecting on their own cognitive processes, a more didactic style is indicated.

However, as I mentioned briefly earlier, you will probably need to use both disputing styles with most of your clients. What happens most often in REBT is that you will start with Socratic disputing and use didactic explanations to supplement your work. Here is a typical sequence of disputing that you will hear in the work of Albert Ellis, the founder of REBT (Yankura & Dryden, 1990).

Client: I must do well in my exams.

Therapist: Why do you have to do well?

[Socratic question]

Client: Because if I don't, my parents will feel let down.

Therapist: That's why it's unpreferable. But just because it is unpreferable if you don't do well, how does it follow that you must do well?

96

[A very brief didactic point followed by another Socratic question]

Client: Because I won't get a very good job later.

Therapist: But again that proves that it would be undesirable if you don't do well. You're saying, though, that you must do well. Now if there was a law of the universe that said that you had to do well, you would have to do well because you would have to follow that law of the universe. Now does that law of the universe exist?

[The therapist realises that the client isn't grasping the point when it is presented Socratically so he or she makes greater use of didactic explanation. However, note that at the end of the intervention, the therapist asks another Socratic question to encourage the client to reflect actively on the point that was presented didactically.]

Module 9
Examples of Albert Ellis's Disputing Work

In this module, I will provide and comment on therapeutic work carried out by Albert Ellis disputing the irrational beliefs of three of his clients. Each sequence focuses on a particular argument.

Unit 32: Using empirical arguments

In this sequence Ellis is disputing the irrational belief of a client who insists that she absolutely must succeed in her career using primarily empirical arguments.

Ellis: Why MUST you have a great career?

Client: Because I very much want to have it.

Ellis: Where is the evidence that you MUST fulfil this strong desire?

Client: I'll feel much better if I do.

Ellis: Yes, you probably will. But how does your feeling better prove that you must succeed?

[So far, Ellis has been using Socratic-type questions. Note how he takes the client's answers to his questions which represent evidence in support of her rational belief (i.e. 'I want to have a great career, but I don't have to have one') and asks whether or not such evidence supports her irrational belief.]

Client: But that's what I want more than anything else in the world.

Ellis: I'm sure you do. But if we take 100 people like you, all of whom want a great career, want it more than anything else in the world, and would feel much better if they achieved it, do they all HAVE to succeed at it?

[Here Ellis probably realises that he has to use a different type of argument with this client. So he asks whether or not it is empirically true

98

that 100 people who have the same strong preference as the client would all change this into a must.]

Client: If they are to have any joy in life, they have to do so.

[The client still does not get the point that Ellis is implying through his Socratic-type questions.]

Ellis: Really? Can't they have ANY pleasure if they fail to get a great career?

[Taking the lead from the client's last response, Ellis changes the focus of his argument again. If 100 people all must have a great career, none of them will have any pleasure if they don't achieve it. Ellis then questions whether this is empirically the case.]

Client: Well, yes. I guess they can have SOME pleasure.

[This is the first time that the client shows any sign that she can think rationally about the issue at hand. Note how Ellis capitalises on this.]

Ellis: And could some of them have a great deal of pleasure?

Client: Um. Probably, yes?

Ellis: Probably?

Client: Well, highly probably.

Ellis: Right. So, no matter how much people greatly want success and would feel better about gaining it, they don't have to get it. Right?

[Here Ellis summarises the rational point and asks for agreement. I might have asked, 'What do you think of this idea?', in order to encourage the client to be more independent in her thinking.]

Client: Well, yes.

Ellis: Reality is that way — isn't it?

Client: It seems so.

Ellis: Back to you. Does YOUR great desire for a successful career mean that you ABSOLUTELY MUST achieve it — that the world HAS TO fulfil this desire?

[Having got the rational point over in an abstract way, Ellis then seeks to apply it to the client's own specific set of personal circumstances.]

Client: I see what you mean. Reality is the way it is, no matter how unpleasant I find it to be.

[The client shows signs of really understanding Ellis's point.]

Ellis: Exactly. Make a note of that Effective New Philosophy you just arrived at and keep thinking that way until you thoroughly believe it!

Unit 33: Using logical arguments

In this segment Ellis is disputing the irrational beliefs of a client who insists that because he treated his friend very nicely and fairly, this friend ABSOLUTELY SHOULD treat him the same way. He does so using primarily logical arguments.

Ellis: Let's suppose that you're describing the situation with your friend accurately and that he treats you shabbily and unfairly after you consistently treat him well. How does it follow that because of your good behaviour he has to respond in kind?

Client: But he's unfair if he doesn't!

Ellis: Yes, we're agreeing on that. He IS unfair and you are fair. Can you jump from 'Because I'm very fair to him, he HAS TO BE fair to me?'

Client: But he's wrong if he isn't fair when I am.

[At this point Ellis and the client appear to be at cross-purposes. Ellis keeps asking the client why his friend MUST be fair to him and the client keeps replying that his friend is wrong and unfair which Ellis is not questioning.]

Ellis: Agreed. But because you are fair, and presumably right, and because he takes advantage of your unfairness, does it STILL follow that he has to be right and to treat you fairly?

Client: It logically follows.

Ellis: Does it? It looks like a complete *non sequitur* to me.

Client: How so?

[This is a typical Ellis change of emphasis. He asserts that the client's belief is illogical and waits for the latter to ask why before expanding on his theme. He wants to get his client into an enquiring, 'Why do you say that?' mode.]

Ellis: Well, it's logical or consistent that he preferably should treat you fairly when you treat him well. But aren't you making an illogical — or 'magical' — jump from 'Because he PREFERABLY should treat me fairly he ABSOLUTELY HAS TO do so?' What 'logical' law of the universe leads to your 'He absolutely has to do so?'

Client: No law, I guess.

Ellis: No, in logic we get necessitous conclusions, such as 'If all men are human and John must be a man, John must be human.' But your 'logic' says, 'People who get treated fairly, often treat others fairly; I treat my friend fairly; therefore it is absolutely NECESSARY that he treat me similarly.' Is that a logical conclusion?

[This is another typical Ellis strategy. He begins by making a point in didactic fashion. As occurs here, this point illustrates a rational idea (in this case a logical idea). He then contrasts this with the client's irrational idea (in this case an illogical idea), but does not tell the client that his idea is illogical. Rather he encourages the client to think for himself by asking, 'Is that a logical conclusion?'. It is worth studying this sequence in detail because it is so typical of Ellis's effective disputing work.]

Client: I guess not.

Ellis: Moreover, you seem to be claiming that because you act fairly and your friend behaves unfairly, his ACTS make him a ROTTEN PERSON. Is that logical thinking?

[Ellis infers other-downing from his client's must. He is probably correct; however, my practice is to check my hunch with the client before proceeding.]

Client: Why not?

[As you will see, Ellis immediately answers the client's question. I would have encouraged the client to make a stab at answering his own question before going into didactic mode.]

Ellis: It's illogical because you're over-generalising. You're jumping from one of his rotten BEHAVIOURS — or even one of his TRAITS — to categorising HIM, his totality as 'rotten'. How does that over-generalisation follow from a few of his behaviours?

[Here Ellis states the logical error that the client is making, shows him in what way the error is present in his belief about his friend and finally questions him about the logicality of that belief.]

Client: I can see now that it doesn't.

Ellis: So what could you more logically conclude instead?

[Here, Ellis encourages the client to be active in his thinking.]

Client: Well, I could think that he isn't one of his main behaviours. He is a person who often, but not always, acts rottenly.

Ellis: Good! Alfred Korzybski and his followers in General Semantics would approve of your new conclusion!

Unit 34: Using pragmatic arguments

In the following piece of work, the client insists that if she believes that she must do well, she will succeed better at school and win others' approval. Ellis shows her that her irrational belief will in all probability produce poor results.

Client: If I am anxious about doing poorly at school because, as you say, I think that I must do well, won't my must and my anxiety motivate me to do better?

Ellis: Yes, in part. But won't they also defeat you?

[Here Ellis gives a straight answer to the client's straight question. But he then follows up by asking a question to encourage the client to think about the issue for herself. This is another typical Ellis disputing strategy.]

Client: How so?

Ellis: If you keep making yourself very anxious with 'I must do well! I must perform perfectly!' won't you preoccupy yourself so much that you DETRACT from the time and energy you can give to studying?

[Yet another typical Ellis intervention. Here Ellis is really making a statement in the guise of a question. The question format is to encourage the client's active participation, but the rational point that Ellis is making is clear.]

Client: Maybe. But I'll still feel quite motivated.

Ellis: Mainly motivated to obsess! You'll be DRIVEN to study. And while you drive yourself, you'll keep thinking, 'But suppose I fail! Wouldn't that be AWFUL?' You'll worry about what your texts will be like, how you will handle them, how you will subsequently perform, etc. How will keeping the future so much in mind help you focus on the PRESENT studying?

[This intervention comprises a number of didactically made points with the question twist at the end.]

Client: It may not help.

Ellis: No, it's much more likely to sabotage. Moreover, even if you somehow succeed in your courses, do you want to be miserably anxious and depressed, WHILE you are succeeding?

Client: Frankly, no.

Ellis: And do you want to be SO absorbed in worrying about school that you have little time for relationships, sports, music and other enjoyments?

[Having succeeded in getting the point across to the client that her irrational belief will do her more harm than good, Ellis spends time — cf. his last two interventions and much of his following responses — underscoring this important point.]

Client: I don't think so. I passed my courses last term but was able to do little else.

Ellis: See! And what about the physical results of your constant worry and perfectionism?

Client: My physician thinks they are making my digestive tract hyperactive.

Ellis: I'm not surprised. And when you constantly worry, how do you feel about YOU for being such a worrier?

Client: Pretty shitty.

Ellis: Is THAT feeling worth it? But even if you felt bad about your anxiety and didn't put YOURSELF down for having it, you would still bring on endless frustration and disappointment by indulging in it.

Client: You may be right.

Ellis: Don't take my word for it. Look for yourself at the results you get from your perfectionistic demands and figure out what you could say to yourself to replace them.

[Ellis often urges his clients not to take his word for it. However, his didactic style does encourage clients not used to thinking for themselves to do just that. Greater extended use of Socratic disputing would achieve this result more effectively.]

Client: Well, I could tell myself, 'It's great to do well at school, but I DON'T HAVE TO BE PERFECT. Even if my anxiety sometimes helps me to get good marks, it, too, has too many disadvantages and it isn't worth it.'

Ellis: Good! That's a much better way to think.

Module 10
Helping Your Client to Understand The Rationality of His Rational Beliefs

In addition to helping your client understand the irrationality of his irrational beliefs, you need to encourage him to understand the rationality of his rational beliefs. By Socratic or didactic means you need to help him to acknowledge the following.

Unit 35: Preferences

Empirical Argument: Your client's rational preferences are consistent with the internal reality of what she wants. To judge whether or not a person has a preference, look at what she says and how she acts. If a preference exists, for example, it will motivate her to approach certain things and to avoid others and this can be observed empirically. Holding a preference is also consistent with reality because it does allow for the person not getting what he wants.

Thus, Victor can provide evidence for his healthy preference: 'I would prefer my boss not to disapprove of me, but there is no reason why he must not do so'. It is consistent with the internal reality of what he wants and you can determine if this is the case by studying how he thinks, talks and acts. Also his rational belief is consistent with reality because it allows for the possibility that his boss may disapprove of him.

Logical Argument: Your client's specific preference follows logically from her general philosophy of preferring to get what she wants. Thus, Victor's specific preference for not having his boss's disapproval follows logically from his general preference of getting what he wants.

Pragmatic Argument: Your client's preferences are more likely to help her to achieve her goals and less likely to lead to psychological disturbance than her musts. Thus, Victor's preference about not having his boss's disapproval will more likely result in him achieving his goal of feeling concerned but not anxious about such disapproval than will his must.

Unit 36: Anti-awfulising

As mentioned in Dryden (1995), an anti-awfulising philosophy involves your client making flexible evaluations (from 0%–99.99%) on a continuum of badness.

Empirical Argument: You can prove that something is bad by looking at the actual or likely consequences for the person concerned. In addition, you can prove that something exists on a continuum of badness by discovering an event that can be worse. Thus, Victor can provide evidence for his anti-awfulising belief: 'It is bad, but not terrible if my boss disapproves of me.' He could argue with justification that if his boss disapproves of him, he is more likely to dismiss Victor and less likely to promote him than if he approves of Victor. Also, Victor can prove his anti-awfulising belief by pointing to situations that would be worse for him than being disapproved of by his boss.

Logical Argument: A person's specific anti-awfulising beliefs make sense in that they point to what the person values and they are also logically related to the broader concept of his general anti-awfulising philosophy. Thus, if Victor believes that it is bad, but not awful when he does not get what he wants (general belief), then it is perfectly logical for him to say that it would be bad, but not awful if his boss disapproved of him (specific belief).

Pragmatic Argument: Anti-awfulising beliefs promote goal achievement. Victor's belief that it is bad, but not awful if his boss disapproves of him will help him to feel concerned, but not anxious about such disapproval. It will also help him to work effectively at his job, thus helping to minimise the chances that he will incur his boss's disapproval.

Unit 37: High frustration tolerance (HFT)

HFT beliefs involve the person believing that she can tolerate difficult life situations and that it is in her interests to do so.

Empirical Argument: HFT beliefs are consistent with reality. It is realistic for Victor to say that he can stand being disapproved of by his boss even though this situation would be difficult for him to tolerate. Indeed, empirically he can prove that he can stand his boss's disapproval even when he irrationally tells himself that he cannot do so. Because, even when he has such an LFT belief, he is standing the situation in that he has neither died nor has he forsaken the possibility of future happiness.

Logical Argument: HFT beliefs are logical. A person's specific HFT beliefs make sense in that they point to what she values and they are also logically related to her broader HFT philosophy. Thus, if Victor believes that he can stand negative events in general, even though he finds it difficult to tolerate them, then it is logical for him to say that whilst he would find it difficult to tolerate, he could stand the specific situation of being disapproved of by his boss.

Pragmatic Argument: HFT beliefs aid goal achievement. If Victor shows himself that he can stand his boss's disapproval even though it would be difficult for him to do so, this belief will help him to feel concerned but not anxious, which is his goal. In addition, his HFT belief will help him to concentrate on his job performance, thus decreasing the chances of him incurring his boss's disapproval.

Unit 38: Self/other-acceptance

Accepting oneself and others as fallible human beings is the healthy alternative to self/other-rating. I will outline the empirical, logical and pragmatic reasons for encouraging clients to endorse self/other-acceptance by taking the example of self-acceptance, although the same arguments can be applied to other-acceptance.

Empirical Argument: Accepting oneself as a fallible human being is consistent with reality. Victor can prove that he is human and fallible with positive, negative and neutral aspects. His essence does not change whether his boss approves or disapproves of him.

Logical Argument: It makes sense for Victor to accept himself as a fallible human being even when his boss disapproves of him. It is perfectly logical, therefore, for him to evaluate this disapproval as negative whilst refraining from giving himself a single rating, as in doing so he is rating a part of his experience without rating his whole person. He does not, thus, make the part–whole error.

Pragmatic Argument: Self-acceptance promotes goal achievement. If Victor accepts himself as a fallible human being even though his boss may disapprove of him he is likely to be concerned, rather than anxious about this disapproval. His self-accepting belief will also encourage him to focus on what he is doing at work rather than on what his boss is thinking of him. This will improve his chances of doing well at work which in turn will decrease the chances of his boss disapproving of him.

Whilst I have presented these arguments didactically, I do want to stress that you can help your client to understand these points Socratically as well as didactically.

In conclusion, the purpose of disputing your client's irrational beliefs is to help her to gain intellectual insight into the fact that her irrational beliefs are inconsistent with reality, illogical and lead to poor psychological results, whereas rational beliefs are empirically based, logical and constructive. Don't expect that once she sees this, she will also have corresponding emotional insight. She won't — yet. In order for her to integrate these concepts so that they make a significant difference to the way she feels and acts, she will need to put them into practice in her everyday life and do so repeatedly using a number of homework assignments. This is the subject of Modules 11 and 12.

Module 11
Negotiating Homework
Assignments

As I mentioned at the end of the previous module, it is important for your client to put into practice in her everyday life what she learns in therapy sessions. In this module, I will discuss several issues that need to be considered when encouraging your client to develop her in-therapy insights.

Unit 39: What's in a name?

Traditionally, REBT therapists call the formal work that clients agree to do between therapy sessions 'homework assignments'. However, it is not envisioned that your client will only do this work 'at home'. Rather, your client will carry out such assignments in whatever extra-therapy context is deemed to be relevant. Thus, the term 'homework assignment' means work that the client agrees to do between therapy sessions. Whilst most of your clients will be happy to use the term 'homework assignment' when discussing with you the work they are prepared to do on themselves between sessions, it is important for you to appreciate that some clients will find this term off-putting.

The main reason for such antipathy concerns the associations that the term 'homework assignment' has with school. In my experience, such clients have negative memories of school in general or homework in particular. For example, one of my clients, Geraldine, associated homework assignments with being locked in her room by her tyrannical mother until she had finished her school homework before being allowed to eat her supper. Not surprisingly, Geraldine reacted negatively to the term 'homework assignment' the first time I used it in counselling. Indeed, she winced visibly at the very mention of the term.

Whilst there has been no research on the relationship between clients' reactions to the term 'homework assignments' and the extent to which they actually carry out such between-session tasks, my clinical experience has been that clients are more likely to carry out such tasks when they use positive (to them) terms to denote these tasks. Given that at least some of your clients will have negative reactions to the term 'homework assignment', it is important that you develop with them terms that have positive connotations.

As a training exercise, pair up with a trainee colleague and develop a list of terms, other than 'homework assignment', that describe the work that your clients need to do between therapy sessions if they are to get the most out of REBT. Do this task before you read the next paragraph.

Here is a brief list of terms that I have used with a sample of my clients who reacted negatively to the term 'homework assignment':

* between-session task;
* change work;
* improvement task;
* goal-achievement task;
* self-help assignment;
* progress assignment.

Having made the point that it is important to use a term that enables your client to construe between-session work positively, I will use the term 'homework assignment' in the remainder of this module for ease of communication.

Unit 40: Discussing the purpose of homework assignments

Bordin (1979) has made the important point that therapeutic tasks need to be goal-directed if their therapeutic potency is to be realised. As discussed in the first volume in this series (Dryden, 1995), one of the most important tasks that your client has to perform in REBT is putting into practice outside therapy what she learns inside therapy. As I have shown above, the best way that she can do this is by carrying out homework assignments. However, as Bordin rightly notes, your client will be unlikely to carry out such assignments if (i) she does not clearly understand the point of doing so in general and (ii) if she does not clearly understand the specific purpose of specific assignments. As I have already dealt with the issue of helping clients understand the importance of carrying out homework assignments in general earlier in this book (see Module 1, Unit 7), I will concentrate here on the importance of helping your clients to understand the specific purpose of given homework assignments.

The most obvious way of doing this is by keeping to the fore of the therapeutic discussion your clients' goals. Here is an example of how to do this.

Windy: So, Barry, can you see that as long as you believe that you must never be rejected you will never ask a girl out for a date?

Barry: Yes, that's self-evident.

Windy: So what's the rational alternative to this belief?

Barry: That I'd rather not be rejected, but there's no reason to assume that I must not be rejected.

Windy: Right. Now, how can you strengthen this belief?

Barry: By asking women out for dates.

Windy: While practising which belief?

Barry: The rational belief that I've just mentioned.

Windy: So do you think it would be a good idea to ask a woman out for a date between now and next week to strengthen this belief?

Barry: OK.

Windy: Will you agree to do this?

Barry: Yes, I will.

Windy: What's the purpose of doing so?

Barry: To get over my anxiety about asking women out on dates and to get used to rejection if it happens.

Windy: That is in fact one of the goals that you mentioned when we discussed what you wanted to gain from counselling. Now, do you think that it would be a good idea to make a note of the homework assignment and the reason why you are going to do it?

Barry: Yes, I do.

Unit 41: Different types of homework assignments

There are different types of homework assignments that you can suggest to your client. I will mention several here, but for a fuller discussion, consult Walen, DiGiuseppe and Dryden (1992).

Cognitive assignments

Cognitive assignments are primarily those which help your client to understand the REBT model and the role that beliefs play in human disturbance and health. They also provide clients with a means of identifying and changing irrational beliefs. Many cognitive assignments are thus structured in a way to help clients use the ABC's of REBT to assess their own problems and use disputing techniques to challenge and change their irrational beliefs. Normally, on their own, such assignments help clients to gain intellectual insight rather than emotional insight into rational principles. They thus serve a very important role in the initial and early-middle stages of therapy.

Many of the assessment techniques that I covered in Volume 1 of this series (Dryden, 1995) and the material that I have presented in Modules 5–8 in this volume can be adapted or tailored for client self-help use. Indeed, I will cover some of the main cognitive techniques that are used in REBT and their self-help variants in Volume 4 of this series. Given this, I will illustrate only two types of cognitive techniques here.

Reading assignments

Reading assignments are mainly cognitive in nature in that your client will gain cognitive understanding from such material. Such assignments are frequently known as bibliotherapy. There is a plethora of self-help books that cover different client problems from an REBT perspective. Initially, you will want to suggest that your client reads a text which introduces basic REBT principles. This may be best done after you have taught your client the ABC's of REBT (see Module 4 in Dryden, 1995).

Howard Young (in Dryden, 1989) noted that clients are generally impressed if you suggest that they read a text or an article that you have written yourself and he thinks that doing so increases the chances that they will read the material. Whilst this awaits empirical investigation, it does make sense and for this reason I frequently suggest that my clients read *Think Your Way to Happiness* which outlines the basic principles of REBT and how these can be applied to common emotional problems (Dryden and Gordon, 1990). If my client expresses alarm at the thought of reading an entire book then I will suggest that he starts with the first chapter or that he reads a condensed booklet version entitled *Think Rationally: A Brief Guide to Overcoming Your Emotional Problems* (Dryden & Gordon, 1992).

Of course, different clients will benefit from reading different introductory material and it is worthwhile becoming familiar with different introductory self-help REBT material so that you can suggest suitable reading material. These range from the simple, e.g. *A Rational Counseling Primer* by Howard Young (1974), to the linguistically complex, e.g. *A New Guide to Rational Living* by Albert Ellis and Bob Harper (1975), which is written in E-prime where no form of the verb 'to be' is employed.

Later you might suggest that your client reads books or articles that are devoted to his specific emotional problems. Paul Hauck has specialised in books on specific themes which are clear and easy to read.

He has written books on anger (Hauck, 1980), assertion (Hauck, 1981a), depression (Hauck, 1974) and anxiety (Hauck, 1981b) amongst others. I have written specific books on sulking (Dryden, 1992) and guilt (Dryden, 1994c).

Another way of approaching rational-emotive bibliotherapy is to suggest that your client reads a book on one or both of the two major forms of psychological disturbance (i.e. ego disturbance and discomfort disturbance). Hauck (1991) has written a book on ego disturbance issues entitled *Hold Your Head Up High* and Jack Gordon and I have written a book devoted to discomfort disturbance issues entitled *Beating the Comfort Trap* (Dryden and Gordon, 1993).

Whichever books or articles you recommend to your client, it is important to note that the purpose of bibliotherapy is to encourage your client to develop intellectual insight into rational principles. Many clients believe that if they read and re-read articles and books on REBT then they will not only understand these principles but will automatically be able to internalise them into their behavioural and emotional repertoire. As I discussed in Module 1, Unit 7, it is very unlikely that this will happen, as internalisation of rational beliefs will usually only occur as a result of repeated cognitive, emotive AND behavioural practice.

Here are three training exercises that will help you to make effective use of bibliotherapeutic materials.

1. Suggest to your trainee colleagues that you each review three different REBT self-help books. In doing so, briefly summarise the content of these books and develop a list of indications and contra-indications for their use. This exercise will allow you and your colleagues (a) to compile a growing list of REBT reading resources and when they can best be used and (b) to develop your powers of criticism in relation to this material.
2. Begin to write your own REBT self-help material. This will enable you to increase your credibility with your clients as well as helping them to 'hear your voice' in the material that they read. I have found that when my clients say that they can 'hear my voice' in the books that I have written, then this helps to reinforce their within-therapy learning.
3. Pair up with a trainee colleague and as therapist help your 'client' to understand the purposes of reading assignments and, as importantly, the limits of bibliotherapy. As elsewhere, tape record the interchange and play it to your REBT trainer or supervisor for feedback.

Listening assignments

Reading assignments obviously involve your client using his or her visual mode of experience. Some clients, however, may not process information readily using this mode. Others may be blind or find reading the small print of self-help books or articles difficult because of failing eyesight. Given these points you will need to offer such clients a plausible and effective alternative mode of communication whereby important rational principles are conveyed.

Using the auditory mode of communication is the obvious alternative here and there are two major types of listening assignments that you can suggest your client does between sessions. First, you can suggest that your client listen to one or more of the numerous audiotapes that are put out by the Institute for Rational-Emotive Therapy (for a catalogue write c/o 45 East 65th Street, New York, NY 10021, USA). Most of these tapes are in the form of lectures on client problems (such as anxiety, anger, depression and procrastination) and how these can be tackled using the principles of REBT.

Second, you can suggest that your client listens to an audio-recording of her therapy sessions. Numerous clients report that they find listening to such recordings helpful. They frequently say that points that they did not quite understand during a therapy session became quite clear on later auditory review. There are three reasons why this might be the case. As a training exercise see if a small group of your trainee colleagues can identify them. You may well discover additional reasons. Do this exercise before reading further.

I hope that you were able to discover the three reasons which I will now discuss.

(i) During therapy sessions, your client may be distracted by her own thoughts and feelings related to the problem that she is discussing with you. Such thoughts and feelings will interfere with her ability to process adequately the points you are trying to convey to her using Socratic or didactic means. On later review and freed from the distracting nature of these thoughts and feelings, your client may well be more able to focus on what you were saying than when you said it at the time.

(ii) During therapy sessions, your client may be reluctant to tell you that she does not understand what you are trying to convey to her. Even when you ask her for her understanding of the points you have been making*, her correct response may belie her true understanding. On later review, and freed from the self-imposed pressure to understand what you are saying, she may, paradoxically, understand more fully than at the time the rational principles you were explaining.

(iii) When your client comes to listen to the recording of her therapy session, she can replay the entire session or segments of it as many

---

*If you recall, I have urged you to do this especially when you have been presenting points didactically (see Module 7).

times as she chooses. Unless she asks you to repeat points several time in the session (which the vast majority of clients will not do), your client only gets to hear once what you say in the therapy session. Repeated review of the entire session or salient segments of the session will often facilitate client understanding of rational principles.

Whenever I suggest that clients review recordings of therapy sessions, I suggest that they make written notes as this encourages them to be active in the reviewing process. I particularly ask them to note points that they found most salient and points which they could not understand even after repeated review. I stress that this is most probably attributable to my deficits as a communicator rather than their deficits in understanding what I was trying to convey.

Another benefit of encouraging clients to listen to recordings of their therapy sessions is that it helps them to re-orientate the therapy. Clients sometimes say, for example, that on reviewing the session they realised that they were not discussing what they really wanted to discuss or that they had omitted important information while discussing salient issues. In this way, your client may well help you to get therapy back on the most important track.

Of course, not all clients will find such listening assignments valuable. In particular, your client may well say that she felt worse after listening to a therapy session than before reviewing it. If this happens regularly, it may well be a sign that you need to suspend the use of this type of homework assignment. Common reasons for clients feeling worse after listening to recordings of therapy sessions usually centre on self-downing issues. Clients may say such things as:

* 'I hated the sound of my voice' (and implicitly — I put myself down for the way I sounded);
* 'I hated myself for sounding so pathetic';
* 'I couldn't believe how stupid I was for not understanding what you were saying'.

Whilst you may be able to encourage your client to practise self-acceptance while listening to facets of herself that she didn't like, most often you will find it more profitable to suspend 'audiotherapy' until your client has made more progress on her self-downing issues. Here as elsewhere in REBT it is important to be flexible.

Imagery assignments

When your client uses imagery assignments, she makes use of both her cognitive and affective modalities. Imagery assignments are obviously cognitive, although they draw on a different part of the brain to that which processes verbal information. They are also affective in nature because visual images, particularly clear images, are affect laden when they embody inferences that are central in the client's personal domain (see Dryden, 1994b)

Imagery assignments can be used by your client between sessions as an assessment tool to identify irrational beliefs that are likely to underpin her predicted disturbed feelings in forthcoming situations. They can also be used by your client as a way of gaining practice in changing unhealthy negative feelings to their healthy counterparts by changing her irrational beliefs to rational beliefs. The important point that your client needs to bear in mind here is keeping the A constant. Otherwise she may learn that she can change her feelings by changing the actual or inferred A. As I showed in the first volume in this series (Dryden, 1995) belief-based change is regarded in REBT as more enduring than inference-based or environmental change.

A third way that your client can employ imagery assignments is as a form of mental rehearsal before carrying out behavioural assignments. Here your client is advised to practise seeing herself in her mind's eye perform poorly as well as adequately. The purpose of encouraging your client to picture herself performing poorly is to help her to think rationally about such an eventuality. Preparing clients for failure as well as success is a typical REBT strategy.

I will deal with some of the most frequently used REBT imagery techniques in Volume 4 of this series. However, I do want to make the point that whilst clients differ markedly in their ability to visualise clearly, a more important factor than image clarity in determining the employment of imagery assignments is the presence of client affect accompanying their use. In my view, such assignments are less useful with clients who experience no affect while picturing themselves in situations where they would in reality feel a lot of emotion than with clients who do experience affect while using imagery.

Behavioural assignments

Behavioural assignments involve your client doing something to counteract his irrational beliefs and to consolidate his rational beliefs. They are assignments which, in the words of Brian Kelly, an Irish REBT therapist, encourage your client to act on his preferences. Given this, behavioural assignments are often used simultaneously with cognitive assignments which provide your client with an opportunity to challenge and change his irrational beliefs. The main purpose of behavioural assignments, then, is to strengthen his conviction in his rational beliefs. I will discuss fully the major REBT behavioural assignments in Volume 4 of this series.

Emotive assignments

Emotive assignments are therapeutic tasks that fully engage your client's emotions. As such, as long as they meet this criterion, certain cognitive and behavioural techniques can be regarded as emotive assignments.

Thus, Ellis regards certain cognitive techniques as emotive in nature when they are employed by the client with force and energy and he sees certain behavioural techniques such as 'shame-attacking exercises' as emotive because the client is encouraged to do certain 'shameful' things and simultaneously 'attack' his shame by disputing the irrational beliefs that underpin this emotion. In addition, certain imagery methods, such as rational-emotive imagery, can be classified as emotive assignments because they attempt to engage fully the client's emotions. I will discuss 'shame-attacking exercises', rational-emotive imagery and the other main REBT emotive techniques more fully in Volume 4 of this series.

As with behavioural assignments, the major purpose of emotive assignments is to help your client to turn his intellectual conviction in his rational beliefs into emotional conviction (see Module 1, Unit 7).

Unit 42: The importance of negotiating homework assignments

The field of behavioural medicine has focused much attention on the factors associated with patient compliance with prescriptive medical treatment. However, the term 'compliance' is an unfortunate one when used in counselling and psychotherapy as it conjures up the image of an all-knowing therapist telling the ignorant client what to do, with the client either complying or not complying with these instructions. Whilst it is debatable whether this image is even appropriate in the field of medicine, it is certainly unsuitable in the field of psychotherapy in general and REBT in particular.

On the other hand, the image of equal collaboration between therapist and client is also not appropriate in REBT. Whilst the egalitarian-collaborative model of the therapeutic relationship is appealing to therapists who view their main role as encouraging the client to use his or her own resources, it is viewed as dishonest by REBT therapists. It ignores, for example, the fact that as an REBT therapist you know more than your client about (i) the nature of psychological disturbance; (ii) how clients, in general, perpetuate their psychological problems and (iii) the processes of therapeutic change and how to facilitate it. Having this knowledge does not entitle you to view yourself as an all-knowing guru and act accordingly, but neither should it lead you to deny that you have such knowledge in the spirit of well-meaning, but ultimately misguided egalitarianism.

As I argued in Volume 1 of this series (Dryden, 1995), REBT theory holds that you and your client are equal in humanity, but unequal in your knowledge and understanding of human disturbance and its remediation. This view of the therapeutic relationship in REBT underpins the importance of negotiating homework assignments with your client. This means that you neither unilaterally tell your client what he will do for homework, nor do you wait for him to tell you what he is going to do between sessions. It means that you will have an informed view concerning the best homework assignment for him at a given time, that you will express this view honestly with your client, but you will very much respect his opinion on the matter and will discuss with him your respective views with the purpose of agreeing a homework assignment to which he will commit himself.

Let me illustrate the differences between the three approaches to homework assignments that I have described. I will first set the scene and then vary the dialogue to highlight these differences.

Windy: So, Norman, you can now see that your anxiety about speaking up in class stems from two beliefs: first, the belief that you must know for certain that you won't say anything stupid and, second, that if you do say something stupid then other people will laugh at you which would prove that you would be stupid through and through. Right?

Norman: Right.

Windy: And the healthy rational alternatives to these two irrational beliefs are?

Norman: That I'd like to be certain that I don't say something stupid, but I don't need this certainty. And I can accept myself as a fallible human being in the event of saying something stupid and people laughing at me.

Windy: Now you also understand that if you want to really believe these two ideas, you need to ...?

Norman: Practise acting according to these two ideas.

1. REBT therapist as unilateral expert: telling a client what he will do for homework

Windy: OK, so what I want you to do between now and next week is to speak up five times in class, and practise your two rational ideas before, during and after doing this. Agreed?

Norman: ...(pause)...(very hesitantly)...A-A-Agreed.

[As you can see, here I have unilaterally decided what is good for my client and I have told him what I want him to do. As the very hesitant response of my client shows, he is most unlikely to do this homework or, if he does, it will be out of fear.]

2. REBT therapist as laissez-faire egalitarian: waiting for your client to tell you what he will do for homework

Windy: So, Norman, what can you do between now and next week to practise and strengthen these two ideas?

Norman: Well, I suppose I can think about the ideas once a day.

Windy: OK, fine.

[Here, because I am overly keen to encourage my client to use his own resources, I do not query his own suggestion. Whilst the client may well carry out this assignment, he will not derive much benefit from it, primarily because it is not a behavioural task.]

3. REBT therapist as authoritative egalitarian: negotiating a homework assignment with your client

Windy: Now, Norman, let me make a suggestion about what you can do to strengthen these beliefs and then we can discuss it. OK?

Norman: Fine.

Windy: First of all, it is important to do something active to get over your fear. Can you see why?

Norman: Because if I don't, I won't overcome it.

Windy: Right, so how about speaking up in class while showing yourself before, during and after you do so that you'd like to be certain that you don't say something stupid, but you don't need this certainty. And that you can accept yourself as a fallible human being in the event of saying something stupid and people laughing at you?

Norman: OK, that sounds reasonable.

Windy: How about speaking up every college day between now and then?

Norman: That's five days! That seems a bit steep.

Windy: What would you suggest?

Norman: Twice?

Windy: How about a compromise of three or four?

Norman: Three it is then.

[Note that here I have taken an authoritative stance by selecting for Norman a relevant behavioural task. However, I am egalitarian in that I ask him for feedback on my suggestion and I am prepared to negotiate a compromise. I thus show that I respect his opinion, but I also ask him to respect mine. My hypothesis is that the client is more likely to carry out this task than he would in the first scenario discussed above when I unilaterally told him what he was to do for homework.]

Unit 43: The 'challenging, but not overwhelming' principle of homework negotiation

Albert Ellis (1983) has been openly critical of many popular behaviour therapy techniques that are based on the principle of gradual desensitisation. Ellis argues that the use of such techniques is inefficient in that it needlessly prolongs the length of therapy and that it tends to reinforce clients' philosophy of low frustration tolerance. By using gradual desensitisation methods it is as if the therapist is implicitly saying to the client: 'You really are a delicate flower who can tolerate virtually no anxiety or discomfort and that is why we will have to take things very gradually.'

Given this, Ellis argues that clients can help themselves best by doing homework assignments based on the principle of flooding or full exposure. Here, your client would practise strengthening his rational beliefs by seeking out situations in which he would be most anxious. He would then stay in these situations until he has strengthened his rational beliefs to the extent that he no longer feels anxiety. He would then do this frequently and repeatedly until he has overcome his problem. Ellis (1985) describes a case where he helped a woman overcome her lift phobia by full exposure methods. The woman agreed to travel repeatedly in lifts in a short period of time until she could travel in them without anxiety. It goes without saying that the client needs to be very motivated to do this. Thus, Ellis's client had just been offered a desired job at the top of a New York skyscraper. Because it was impossible for her to take the stairs, she was faced with the choice of declining the position or travelling in the lift to her new office.

When clients have such motivation and are prepared to tolerate the high levels of discomfort to which flooding methods lead, you should encourage them to undertake homework assignments based on the principle of full exposure. However, in my experience, most clients will not agree to carry out such assignments. In such instances, is there a better alternative to homework assignments based on gradual desensitisation? The answer is yes and these are assignments based on the principle that I have called 'challenging, but not overwhelming'. Such assignments occupy a middle ground between flooding and gradual desensitisation methods. They constitute a challenge for the client, which if undertaken would lead to therapeutic progress, but would not be overwhelming for the client (in his judgment) at that particular time. Here is an example of how I introduce this concept to clients.

Windy: Now, Norman, how quickly do you want to overcome your fear of speaking up in class: very quickly, moderately quickly or slowly?

Norman: Very quickly.

Windy: And how much discomfort are you prepared to face in overcoming your problem: great discomfort, moderate discomfort or no discomfort?

Norman: Well, ideally no discomfort.

Windy: So you'd like to overcome your problem very quickly and without discomfort. Right?

Norman: Right.

Windy: Well, I'd really like to help you to do that but, unfortunately, I can't. Let me explain. If you want to overcome your problem very quickly, you will have to speak up in class very frequently and this will involve you tolerating much discomfort. Here you will have to do assignments based on the principle of full exposure. However, if you want to experience minimal levels of discomfort, then it follows that you will have to go very slowly. Here you will do assignments based on the principle of gradual desensitisation. A middle ground between these two positions is based on the principle that I call 'challenging, but not overwhelming'. Here you will choose to do homework assignments that are challenging, but not overwhelming for you at any point in time. This would involve you tolerating moderate levels of discomfort and would lead you to make progress moderately quickly. Is that clear?

Norman: Yes. You're saying that I can go slowly, moderately quickly or very quickly. The quicker I decide to go, the more discomfort I will have to tolerate.

Windy: That's exactly right. So, how would you like to proceed?

Norman: According to the 'challenging, but not overwhelming' principle.

Windy: Then let's see what you can do between now and next week that will allow you to practise strengthening your rational beliefs in a way that is challenging for you...

Let me make two concluding remarks on this issue.

1. I tend to dissuade any clients who say that they wish to follow the 'gradual desensitisation' route. I point out to them that doing so will be counterproductive in that taking this route will tend to reinforce their philosophy of low frustration tolerance. However, I do not insist that such clients begin with 'challenging, but not overwhelming' homework assignments. If the worst comes to the worst, I would start with the 'gradual desensitisation' route, hoping to 'transfer' them to the 'challenging, but not overwhelming' route as quickly as possible.
2. A number of clients who begin by carrying out 'challenging, but not overwhelming' homework assignments do switch to flooding-type assignments after they have made some progress and they get accustomed to tolerating moderate levels of discomfort.

In the following units, I want to mention a number of principles that you can follow to increase the chances that your client will carry out his jointly negotiated homework assignment. Please note, however, that none of these methods will guarantee that he will actually do the assignment. Assuming that you have carried out the following steps, it is important not to lose sight of the fact that your client is ultimately responsible for whether or not he will do his homework. Thus, whether he does so or not, it is not a measure of your worth as a therapist (or even as a person!).

Unit 44: Teach your client the 'no-lose' concept of homework assignments

The 'no lose' concept of homework assignments is designed to give your client additional encouragement to agree to carry out an assignment. While introducing the concept to your client you need to stress that there is no way that your client can lose if he agrees to undertake the homework task, and you need to emphasise three points as shown in the following dialogue.

Windy: So to recap, Norman, you have agreed to speak up in class on three occasions while showing yourself (i) that you don't need to be certain that you won't say anything stupid before you speak and (ii) that if you do say something stupid you can still accept yourself as a fallible human being even if people in your seminar group laugh at you. Is that right?

Norman: Well, I'm still a bit doubtful about it.

Windy: I can appreciate that, but let me put it this way. If you undertake to do the assignment, then there is no way you can lose. Do you know why?

Norman: No, why?

Windy: Well, let me put it like this. First, if you agree to do the assignment and you actually do it and it works out well, then that's good because you have made a big stride forward in meeting your goals. Right?

Norman: Yes, I can see that.

Windy: Second, if you agree to do the assignment and you actually do it, but it doesn't go well, then that's valuable because we can analyse what happened and you can learn from the experience. Do you see that?

Norman: Yes, I do.

Windy: And finally, if you undertake to do the homework assignment, but you don't do it, then that is also valuable. Do you know why?

Norman: ...Because we can find out how I stopped myself from doing it?

Windy: That's right. We can discover obstacles which neither of us knew about and then we can help you to overcome them. So, can you see why if you agree to do the assignment, you can't lose.

Norman: Very good. You should be a salesman!

Windy: I am. I'm trying to sell you on the concept of mental health and how you can achieve it!

Unit 45: Ensure that your client has sufficient skills to carry out the homework assignment

It is important that your client has the skills to carry out the negotiated homework assignment. For example, if you have suggested that he complete a written ABC form, it is important that you first instruct him in its use. He is more likely to do the assignment if he knows what to do than if he doesn't.

Unit 46: Ensure that your client believes that he can do the homework assignment

Self-efficacy theory (Bandura, 1977) predicts that your client is more likely to carry out a homework assignment if he believes that he can actually do it than if he lacks what Bandura calls an 'efficacy expectation'. Given this, it is important to spend some time helping your client to see that he is able to carry out the homework task. One way to do this is to suggest that your client uses imagery techniques where he repeatedly pictures himself carrying out the assignment before he does so in reality.

It is important to distinguish between an efficacy expectation and the more objective question of whether or not your client has a particular skill in his repertoire. It is possible that your client has a skill in his repertoire but subjectively believes that he is unable to use this skill in a particular setting. Thus, it is insufficient to teach your client a skill such as filling in a written ABC form (see point 1 above). You also need to help him to develop the relevant efficacy expectation.

Windy: So do you think you can speak up in class while showing yourself that you don't need to be certain that you won't say anything stupid and that you can accept yourself as a fallible human being if you do?

Norman: I'm not sure.

Windy: Well let's see. Close your eyes and picture yourself in class. Have you got that image in mind?

Norman: Yes, I have.

Windy: Good. now see yourself showing yourself that you don't need to be certain that you won't say anything stupid and that you can accept yourself as a fallible human being if you do. Have you got that?

Norman: Yes.

Windy: Now keep those two beliefs in mind and see yourself speaking up in class. Can you do that?

Norman: Yes, I can picture that.

Windy: So does this show you that you can do this assignment in reality?

Norman: Yes, it does.

Unit 47: Give yourself sufficient time to negotiate a homework assignment

I have listened to many therapy sessions conducted by beginning REBT therapists over the years and I have been struck by how little time such therapists allocate to negotiating homework assignments with their clients. They frequently leave the issue of homework to the very last minute with the result that they end up by telling their clients what they want them to do between sessions. Because negotiating a suitable assignment takes time, I suggest that you allocate ten minutes to this activity. This will enable you to incorporate all of the issues that I have discussed in this module which, I argue, will increase the chances that your client will execute the homework task successfully.

If you have negotiated a suitable homework assignment in the early or middle part of a therapy session you will not need to devote ten minutes to this task at the end of a session. However, it is still worthwhile allocating a few minutes to recap on the homework, otherwise your client may forget what his homework is. This latter point emerged from a book that my colleague, Joseph Yankura, and I did on the therapy work of Albert Ellis entitled *Doing RET: Albert Ellis in Action* (Yankura and Dryden, 1990). We noted that Ellis did not consistently negotiate specific homework assignments with his clients at the end of a session. Ellis replied that he often makes homework suggestions during a therapy session. The important point here is not whether a therapist did or did not negotiate a homework assignment, but whether her clients remember the homework. When we interviewed several of Ellis's clients for the book we came away with the impression that Ellis's clients did not recall that he consistently suggested specific homework tasks. One way to ensure that your client remembers that homework has been negotiated, particularly when this has been discussed in the main body of the session, is to review it at session's end.

Another way of encouraging your client to remember his homework is to suggest that he keeps a written record of the assignment. I will discuss this further in Unit 52 below.

Unit 48: Ensure that the homework assignment follows logically from the work you have done with your client in the therapy session

Much of the work you will do in a therapy session will be focused on one of your client's target problems (see Dryden,1995). Towards the end of the session, you should negotiate a homework assignment with your client that logically follows from the work you have done with him on the target problem. The following is a rough guide of when to negotiate which type of homework assignment.

(a) Negotiate a reading assignment when the work you have done with your client has centred on helping your client to understand the relationship between her unhealthy negative emotion and her irrational beliefs.

(b) Negotiate a written homework assignment (e.g. an ABC form) when the session work has centred on helping your client to identify and dispute her irrational beliefs and when you have trained your client in the use of the relevant written form.

(c) Negotiate an imagery assignment when the session work has focused on beginning to strengthen rational beliefs, but your client is not ready to undertake a behavioural assignment.

(d) Negotiate a behavioural assignment (along with a relevant cognitive disputing technique) when the session work has prepared your

client to strengthen her rational beliefs by 'acting on her preferences'.
(e) Negotiate an emotive assignment when the session has been devoted to discussing how your client can deepen her conviction in her
rational beliefs other than through the use of behavioural assignments.

To reiterate, whatever type of homework assignment you negotiate
with your client, ensure that it is relevant to the work you have done
with her in the session.

Unit 49: Ensure that your client understands the nature and purpose of the homework assignment

I have mentioned this point in Unit 40, but it is so important I wish to
reiterate it here. At the end of the process of homework negotiation, it
is useful to ask your client to summarise the homework assignment
and its rationale. It is particularly important to ensure that your client
has understood the reason why he has agreed to carry out the assignment. My clinical experience has shown me that the more a client
keeps the purpose of a negotiated homework assignment at the fore-
front of his mind, the more likely it is that he will do the agreed assignment.

Windy: So let's recap. What are you going to do between now and next
week?

Norman: I'm going to speak up in class and practise my new rational
beliefs.

Windy: And what's the purpose of speaking up in class while showing
yourself that you don't need to be certain that you won't say anything
stupid and that you can accept yourself as a fallible human being if you
do?

Norman: Well, it will help me to be able to speak up in class whenever
I want to say something without feeling anxious.

Unit 50: Help your client to specify when, where and how often she will do the homework task

If you can help your client to specify the number of times he will carry
out the negotiated homework assignment, when he will do it and in
what setting, then he is more likely to do it than if no such agreements
are made.

Windy: Now, Norman, how many times between now and next week
will you agree to speak up in class while practising your rational

beliefs? I was thinking that four times might be a challenging number, but I don't want to suggest this if it is too overwhelming for you at this point.

[Review the 'challenging, but not overwhelming principle' in Unit 43.]

Norman: Well, that's sounds a bit steep. How about twice?

Windy: Shall we compromise on three?

Norman: OK then.

Windy: And where will you do this?

Norman: Well, I've got four seminars next week. I can do it in three of those.

Windy: Let's be really specific here.

Norman: Well, I can do it in the Monday seminar at 3 pm, in the Wednesday seminar at noon and in the Friday seminar at 10 am.

Windy: Good, now let's talk about when in the seminars you will do this. In my experience it is better to do the homework early in the seminar rather than later. Does that make sense?

Norman: Yes, it does.

Windy: So would it make sense to speak up in the first twenty minutes of the seminar?

Norman: Yes, that makes sense.

Windy: Will you do it?

Norman: Yes.

Unit 51: Elicit a firm commitment that your client will carry out the homework assignment

It is important to get a firm commitment from your client to do the assignment rather than a vague commitment such as 'I think I can do that' or 'I'll try'. When your client makes a definite commitment to do the homework assignment, she is more likely to do it than if she makes a vague commitment.

Windy: So would it make sense to speak up in the first twenty minutes of the seminar?

Norman: OK. I'll try to do that.

Windy: Let me show you the difference between 'do' and 'try'. Snap your fingers...(Norman snaps his fingers)...Now try to snap your fingers, but don't actually snap them...(Norman makes the relevant movement but doesn't actually snap his fingers). Can you see the difference between 'try' and 'do'?

Norman: When you do something you do it. But when you try, it doesn't mean that you will do it.

Windy: So will you commit yourself to speak up in the first twenty minutes or will you commit yourself to trying?

Norman: I'll do it.

Unit 52: Encourage your client to keep a written note of his homework assignment and relevant details

Experienced General Practitioners know that one way of increasing the chances that patients will follow medical advice is to provide them with a written summary of that advice. There are several reasons why a patient may not remember medical advice. First, she may simply forget the advice. Second, the advice may be too complex to be processed properly at the time. Third, the patient may be anxious during the medical consultation and this anxiety may affect her cognitive functioning during and after that consultation.

The same factors may operate during the psychotherapeutic interview and having your client write down the homework assignment or providing her with a written summary of the assignment will increase the chances that she will carry out the assignment. Some REBT therapists keep a supply of 'No Carbon Required' (NCR) paper on which they write or have their clients write down the homework assignment. NCR paper provides an automatic copy for the therapist to keep in his or her files to be retrieved at the beginning of the next session when the therapist will check the client's assignment (see Module 12).

What information should be put on the written record? My practice is to have my client record the following information:

(i)   The nature of the assignment.
(ii) The purpose of the assignment.
(iii) How often the client will carry out the assignment.
(iv) Where the client will carry out the assignment.
(v)   When the client will carry out the assignment.
(vi) Possible obstacles to carrying out the assignment.
(vii) How these obstacles can be overcome.

The above seven sections can be completed by the client at the end of the therapy session in which the homework task has been negotiated. The following three sections are to be completed by the client between therapy sessions:

(viii) What the client actually did.

(ix)   Actual obstacles to carrying out the assignment.

(x)   What the client actually learned from carrying out the assignment.

Here is how Norman completed the first seven sections of the homework form at the end of the therapy session in which the assignment was negotiated.

(i)   The nature of the assignment.

I will speak up in class while showing myself that I don't need to be certain that I won't say anything stupid and that I can accept yourself as a fallible human being if I do.

(ii) The purpose of the assignment.

Doing this will help me to be able to speak up in class whenever I want to say something, without feeling anxious.

(iii) How often the client will carry out the assignment.

Three times.

(iv) Where the client will carry out the assignment.

  (a) Monday seminar at 3 pm;
  (b) Wednesday seminar at noon;
  (c) Friday seminar at 10 am.

(v) When the client will carry out the assignment.

During the first twenty minutes of each seminar.

(vi) Possible obstacles to carrying out the assignment.

Feeling very uncomfortable.

(vii) How these obstacles can be overcome.

I can show myself that I can speak up even though I am feeling very uncomfortable and that if I do speak up the discomfort will probably subside.

Unit 53: Troubleshoot any obstacles that will stop your client from carrying out the homework assignment

It has been my experience that when I have helped my clients to identify potential obstacles to homework completion and to find ways of dealing with these obstacles, then they are more likely to do the home-work than when I have not instituted such troubleshooting. What may serve as potential obstacles to homework completion? Golden (1989) has provided a comprehensive list of such obstacles and I refer the reader to his excellent discussion of the subject. Given this, I will only consider here the most common obstacle which is a philosophy of low frustration tolerance (LFT). Clients often provide many rationalisations in their explanations of why they did not do their homework (e.g. 'I didn't have the time' or 'I forgot') when the real reason can be attrib-uted to LFT (e.g. 'I didn't do the task because I thought I would feel too uncomfortable doing it'). It is thus worthwhile raising LFT as a potential obstacle to homework completion even though your client doesn't mention it. This is what I did with Norman.

Windy: Now, Norman, it is often useful in therapy to troubleshoot any reasons why you might not do what you have agreed to do for home-work. Can you think of any reason why you might not do yours?

Norman: No, I'm pretty sure that I will do it.

Windy: But what if you begin to feel very uncomfortable in the moments before you have decided to speak up?

Norman: Good point. If that happened I might well duck out of doing it.

Windy: What do you think you would need to tell yourself to speak up even though you are feeling uncomfortable?

Norman: That I can speak up even though I am feeling very uncomfort-able and that if I do speak up the discomfort will probably subside.

Windy: Would that work?

Norman: Yes, it would.

Windy: So why not imagine yourself feeling very uncomfortable in the seminar situation and show yourself that you can speak up anyway.

Norman: That's a good idea.

Unit 54: Rehearse the homework assignment in the therapy room

It is often a good idea to rehearse the assignment in the therapy session if this is practicable. If not you can use imagery rehearsal as a plausible substitute. Rehearsing your client's homework assignment in the session serves both to increase his sense that he will be able to do the assign-ment in reality and to identify potential obstacles to homework comple-tion that haven't been identified through verbal discussion of this issue.

Windy: Let's rehearse the assignment briefly. OK?

Norman: OK.

Windy: Shall I play your tutor and perhaps one other student and we can imagine that there are other students present too? Your task is to speak up while practising the two rational beliefs that we discussed. OK?

Norman: Fine.

Windy (as tutor): So this week we are discussing the role of Catholicism in Evelyn Waugh's novel *Brideshead Revisited*. Who would like to kick off?

[I first discovered that this was to be the topic for one of Norman's forthcoming seminars.]

Windy (as student): I think that Waugh shows his deep ambivalence about Catholicism in this novel because several of the characters are at one time scornful of it and at another time drawn towards it.

Norman: I would agree with that. For example, who would have thought that Sebastian would have ended up as he did, as a kind of unpaid janitor in a religious order. And his father ended his life by making the sign of the cross, even though he spent most of his life being openly scornful of Catholicism....

Windy (as therapist): How did that go?

Norman: I did feel a bit anxious, but that went as I got into my stride.

Windy: Do you think this will help you to speak up in the seminar?

Norman: Well, I think I'll be more uncomfortable then, but I'm sure now that I'll be able to do it.

Unit 55: Use the principle of rewards and penalties to encourage your client to do the homework assignment

Sometimes it is helpful to suggest to your client that he can use the principle of rewards and penalties to encourage him to do his homework assignment. Basically this involves your client rewarding himself when he does the assignment and penalising (but not condemning) himself if he fails to do it. This principle can be applied by your client particularly when he may not do the assignment owing to a philosophy of LFT, as in the following example.

Windy: So you still think that you might not do the assignment if you experience a lot of discomfort. Is that right?

Norman: I think so.

Windy: If that happens you can use the principle of rewards and penalties as an added incentive. Here is how it works. What do you like doing every day that you would be very reluctant to give up?

Norman: Reading the newspaper.

Windy: And what do you really dislike doing?

Norman: Cleaning the oven.

Windy: OK. If you speak up in class you can the read the newspaper and you won't have to clean the oven. However, if you don't speak up then you have to clean the oven and no reading the newspaper. Agreed?

Norman: Wow, that's tough.

Windy: That's right. Tough measures for tough problems.

Norman: OK. I doubt whether I'll need to use this principle, but I'll do it if I need what you call an added incentive.

[If your client is going to use the principle of rewards and penalties then have him write this agreement on his homework form.]

Unit 56: Monitor your skills at negotiating homework assignments

I strongly suggest that you monitor your skills at negotiating homework assignments with the purpose of improving these skills. You can do this by tape recording your therapy sessions routinely and using the scale given in Appendix 1 to evaluate your performance. Before you do so, please note that very few therapists will score highly on all of the scale's items. Indeed, some items will not be relevant and there is an opportunity to indicate this on the scale. However, if you do answer 'No' to any item (as opposed to 'Not Appropriate') then write down what you would have done differently given hindsight and what you would have needed to change in order to have answered 'Yes'. As I have suggested throughout this book, take any enduring problems in negotiating homework assignments to your REBT supervisor or trainer.

Module 12
Reviewing Homework
Assignments

In the final module of this volume, I will discuss the issues that arise when you come to review your client's homework. To give you an idea of the important role that reviewing homework assignments plays in the REBT therapeutic process consider the following view of the structure of REBT sessions put forward by Ray DiGiuseppe (personal communication), the Director of Professional Education at the Institute for Rational-Emotive Therapy in New York:

Review Homework
Carry Out Session Work
Negotiate Homework

Reviewing homework when therapy is under way, then, is often the first therapeutic task that you have to perform in a session as an REBT therapist and has a decided bearing on the rest of that session. Let me begin the discussion by outlining the most central principle of reviewing homework.

Unit 57: Put reviewing your client's homework assignment on the session agenda

Reviewing your client's homework conveys to him or her two things. First it shows her that you consider homework assignments to be an integral part of the therapeutic process. If you, as a client, had agreed to carry out a homework assignment and had actually done so, how would you respond if your therapist did not ask for a report on what you did and what you learned from doing the assignment? My guess is that you would not be pleased. Being human, you would also be less likely to carry out future homework assignments than you would be if your therapist had reviewed the homework with you. For that is what I have found as an REBT therapist and supervisor: clients are more likely to do homework assignments when their therapists initiate regular reviews of their previous assignments than when their therapists do not do so. Consequently, the first and perhaps the most important principle of reviewing your client's homework assignments is actually to review them!

The second point that you convey to your client when you review his or her homework is that you are genuinely interested in the therapeutic progress. Earlier in the process of REBT, you will have helped your client to see that homework assignments are an important vehicle for stimulating therapeutic progress by helping him or her to deepen conviction in his or her rational beliefs (Dryden, 1995). In other words doing homework assignments helps your client to go from intellectual to emotional insight. Asking your client about his or her homework assignments shows that you are taking a regular interest in his or her progress on this issue. Failing to review assignments may convey the opposite: that you are indifferent to his or her therapeutic progress.

Unit 58: When is it best to review homework assignments?

Having put reviewing homework assignments on the therapeutic agenda, when is the best time to initiate such a review? In my opinion, the best time to review your client's homework assignments is to do so at the beginning of the next therapy session. If you set a formal, structured agenda for each therapy session with your client as many cognitive therapists do (see Beck et al., 1979), you will put the item 'previous homework' on the agenda for every session. You will also want to suggest placing this item early on the agenda. The reason for this is that what your client did or did not do for homework and what he or she learned or did not learn from doing it will have an important influence on the content of the current session.

On the other hand, if your practice is not to set a formal agenda at the beginning of every session, you will still want to initiate the homework review early in the session. Indeed, some REBT therapists routinely begin each therapy session with an enquiry about their client's previous week's homework. For example, Ed Garcia has a tape in the Institute for RET's professional tape library which begins with him asking his client, 'What did you do for homework?'

There are, of course, exceptions to this principle. For example, if your client comes into the therapy session in a very agitated or even suicidal state, I hope that you would deal with this crisis rather than attempt to review his last homework task! Here, as elsewhere, it is important to practise REBT in a humane, flexible manner.

In the following units, I will outline and discuss several points that you need to consider as you review your client's homework assignment.

Unit 59: When your client states that he did the homework assignment, check whether or not it was done as negotiated

When your client reports that he carried out the homework assignment, the first point to check when you review the homework assignment is whether or not the client did it as negotiated. It may well happen that your client has changed the nature of the assignment and in doing so has lessened the therapeutic potency of the assignment.

You will recall that the homework assignment I negotiated with Norman was as follows:

'I will speak up in three different seminars while showing myself that I don't need to be certain that I won't say something stupid before I speak and that if I do say something stupid I can still accept myself as a fallible human being even if others laugh at me.'

There are a variety of ways in which Norman could have modified the assignment. Here is a selection of the large number of ways in which Norman might have changed the nature of his homework assignment:

(i) Norman could have done the assignment as agreed, but only on one or two occasions rather than the three we negotiated.

(ii) He could have spoken up on three separate occasions, but without practising the new rational beliefs or making any changes to his other distorted cognitions such as his inferences.

(iii) He could have spoken up on three separate occasions while changing his distorted inferences or other unrealistic thoughts rather than practising his new rational beliefs. For example, while speaking up he might have told himself that there was little chance of him saying any thing stupid or, if he did, that people would be on his side rather than against him.

(iv) He could have spoken up on three separate occasions while thinking positive, Pollyanna-ish thoughts such as: 'Every time I speak up I'm getting better and better' or defensive thoughts such as 'It doesn't matter if I say something stupid' or 'It doesn't matter if the people in the seminar group laugh at me if I do something stupid.'

One common way in which your client may change the nature of his negotiated homework assignment is when he does not face the situation that he has agreed to face. In REBT parlance, he has not faced the actual A. For example let's suppose that your client has a fear of being rejected by women when he asks them to dance. In the session you work carefully to identify, challenge and help him to change the irrational belief that underpins his anxiety. Following on from this work you negotiate with him an assignment which involves him practising his new rational belief in the face of actual rejection by a woman. You stress to him that the important aspect of this assignment is not so much asking women to dance, but being rejected by them. Because the client is afraid of rejection, it is important that he faces rejection. At the next session, your client is pleased with the results of his homework. He asked a woman to dance, she accepted his invitation, they spent an enjoyable evening together and they have begun to date. The important point to note from a therapeutic point of view is that the client has not faced the A that he agreed to face. As I will show you below, it is important that you help your client to see that whatever the outcome of his pleasant evening with the aforementioned woman, he has not confronted the source of his problem.

How do you respond when it becomes clear that your client has changed the nature of his homework? I suggest that you do the following:

Step 1: Encourage your client by saying that you were pleased that he did the assignment.

Step 2: Explain how, in your opinion, he changed the assignment and remind him of the exact nature of the task as it was negotiated by the two of you in the previous session. In doing so, if indicated, remind your client of the purpose of the assignment which dictated its precise form.

Step 3: If your client made a genuine mistake in changing the nature of the assignment, invite him to re-do the assignment, but this time as it was previously negotiated. If he agrees, ensure that he keeps a written reminder of the assignment and ask him to guard against making further changes to it. Don't forget to review the assignment in the following session. If he doesn't agree to do the assignment, explore and deal with his reluctance.

Step 4: If it appears that the change that your client made to the assignment was motivated by the presence of an implicit irrational belief, identify and deal with this belief and again invite your client to re-do the assignment as it was previously negotiated, urging him once again to guard against making further change to the assignment. Alternatively, modify the assignment in a way that takes into account the newly discovered obstacle.

Here is an example of how to put this into practice.

Windy: Let's begin by reviewing your homework. How did it go?

Norman: It went fairly well. I managed to speak up on two occasions.

Windy: I'm pleased to hear that. Did you practise the two rational beliefs at the same time?

[See step 1 above]

Norman: Yes, I made sure I did that.

Windy: Good. I'll check what you learned from doing the homework in a moment. But, first, are you aware that you didn't quite do all the homework?

[See step 2 above]

Norman: You mean that I didn't speak up on three occasions?

Windy: Yes, it's important for me to understand what happened on the occasion that you didn't speak up. Can you help me to understand that?

Norman: Well, it was at the Friday morning seminar. I remember feeling quite uncomfortable...but er...I guess I thought that as I'd done quite well I would give myself a break and not speak up on that day.

Windy: I see. You said that you were feeling quite uncomfortable. What exactly was the nature of that feeling?

[Here I am seeking to clarify the client's C (see Dryden, 1995). My hunch is that the client did not do the third part of his assignment because he was thinking irrationally at the time and this led to avoidance — see step 4.]

Norman: I was anxious....

I then proceeded to use inference chaining to discover that Norman was anxious about saying something stupid in front of a female student whom he found attractive and who rarely attended seminars. I then identified and challenged Norman's new irrational belief: 'I must speak well in front of Joanna' and we negotiated a new homework assignment where he would seek out Joanna and have an intellectual discussion with her while practising his new rational belief: 'I'd like to speak well in front of Joanna, but I don't have to do so.' The second assignment that I negotiated with Norman concerned asking Joanna to attend the next seminar and, if she did, he would do the third part of his original homework task. I suggested that Norman ask Joanna to attend the next seminar because, left to her own devices, Joanna would probably not attend another seminar for quite a while.

Unit 60: Review what your client learned from doing the assignment

The next step in the homework-reviewing process concerns asking your client what he learned from doing the homework. If your client learned what you hoped he would learn, acknowledge that he did well and move on. If your client did not learn what you hoped he would learn, then you need to address this issue. Let me show how I dealt with this latter situation with Norman.

Windy: So, Norman, you managed to speak up on the three occasions as we agreed and you were also able to practise strengthening your new rational beliefs. Is that right?

Norman: Yes, that's right.

Windy: Good. Now what did you learn from doing the assignment?

Norman: I learned that it is very unlikely that I will say something stupid in a seminar setting.

Windy: Did you learn anything else?

Norman: No, that's about it.

[The purpose of the homework assignment was to help Norman over his anxiety about speaking up in class. The way Norman and I chose to do this was to have him challenge his irrational beliefs about being certain that he would not say anything stupid before he spoke and about how others viewed him and to have him practise the rational alternatives while speaking up. Ideally, what I would have liked Norman to have learned was that he didn't need to be certain before he spoke and that if others laughed at him if he did say something stupid then he could accept himself as a fallible human being in this situation. However, he did not mention either of these two beliefs in what he learned. Rather, he said that he learned that it was now unlikely that he would say something stupid in class. Whilst this is an important learning, it is based on an inferential change which in REBT theory is considered to lead to less enduring results than belief change (see Dryden, 1995 for a discussion of this point).

Consequently, my task is to explain this to Norman and encourage him to focus on making a change in belief, while not undermining what for him was likely to be a significant piece of learning.]

Windy: I think the fact that you learned that it is unlikely that you will say something stupid in class is important for you and by saying what I am about to say I do not mean to detract from this. OK?

Norman: OK.

Windy: Good. Now when you focused on the idea that you were unlikely to say something stupid how did this help you?

Norman: It got rid of the anxiety and helped me to speak up.

Windy: But how do you know for sure that you won't say something stupid?

Norman: I guess I don't.

Windy: Right, And let's suppose that you do say something stupid and people laugh at you, will the idea that you are unlikely to say something stupid help you to deal productively with that situation?

Norman: No, it won't.

Windy: Now, again, learning that you are unlikely to say something stupid in class is important and note that you did speak up without having a guarantee that you wouldn't say something stupid.

Norman: Right, but as we talk about it, I can see that I wasn't really telling myself that it was unlikely that I would say something stupid. I was telling myself that I definitely wouldn't say something stupid.

Windy: I see. Now that means that if you are to speak up without such guarantees and if you are to cope with people laughing at you then it would be really useful if you could speak up regularly in class and deliberately say something stupid on one or two occasions.

Norman: So that I introduce some uncertainty into the situation you mean?

Windy: Exactly. And so you can deal with the possibility or even actuality of people laughing at you.

Norman: Wow, that's a tough assignment.

Windy: Well, let's see if we can negotiate something challenging, but not overwhelming. The main thing though is for you to learn (1) that you can speak up even when there is the possibility that you may say something stupid and (2) that you can accept yourself as a fallible human being when you do say something stupid and there is a chance that people will laugh at you.

[Norman and I then proceeded to negotiate an assignment using the guidelines discussed in Module 11.]

Unit 61: Capitalise on your client's success

How do you respond when your client has successfully done his homework and has learned what you hoped he would learn? I recommend that you reinforce him for achievement and suggest that he build on his success.

Windy: So, Norman, you were able to speak up on three separate occasions while practising your rational beliefs. and you say that you are beginning to really believe that you don't need certainty that you won't say anything stupid before you speak up and that even if you do say something stupid and people laugh at you, you can accept yourself as a fallible human being in the face of ridicule. Is that right?

Norman: Yes, that's right.

Windy: How do you feel about what you have achieved and what you are learning?

Norman: I feel really good about it.

Windy: I'm pleased. I think you are doing really well...(humorously) Of course that doesn't mean that you are a more worthwhile person!

Norman:...(laughs) Ha, Ha, Ha.

Windy: Seriously though, you are doing well, so let's talk about how you can capitalise on your success. OK?

Norman: OK.

Windy: What do you think you can do between now and next week to extend this?

Norman: Well, I guess I can undertake to speak up at every seminar.

Windy: Good. How about undertaking to speak up at least twice at every seminar you attend?

Norman: (humorously) You're a real taskmaster, aren't you?

Windy: Does that mean yes or no?

Norman: OK, I'll do it.

Windy: Excellent. Let's make a written note of what you're going to do and where and when you are going to do it (see Module 11, Unit 52).

Unit 62: Responding to your client's homework 'failure'

Let's suppose that your client has done her homework, but it turned out poorly. When this happens, clients often say that they did the assignment, but 'it didn't work'. I have put the word 'failure' in inverted commas here because although clients regard the assignment as a 'failure', as shown in Module 11, Unit 44, there is much to learn from this situation. So, when you encounter this so-called 'failure', remind your client of the 'no-lose' nature of homework assignments and begin to investigate the factors involved. But first ask for a factual account about what happened. Then, once you have identified the factors that accounted for the 'failure', help your client to deal with them and endeavour to re-negotiate the same or similar assignment.

While you are investigating the factors which accounted for your client's homework 'failure', it is useful to keep in mind a number of such factors. Here is an illustrative list of some of the more common reasons for homework 'failure'.

* Your client implemented certain, but not all the elements of the negotiated assignment (see this module, Unit 59). For example, your client may have done the behavioural aspect of the assignment, but did not practise new rational beliefs with the result that he experienced the same unhealthy negative emotions associated with the target problem.
* The assignment was 'overwhelming, rather than challenging' for your client at this time.
* Your client began to do the assignment but stopped doing it because he began to experience discomfort which he believed he could not tolerate.
* Your client practised the wrong rational beliefs during the assignment.
* Your client practised the right rational beliefs, but did so in a overly weak manner with the result that his unhealthy negative emotions predominated.
* Your client began to do the assignment, but forgot what he was to do after he had begun.
* Your client began the assignment, but gave up because he did not experience immediate benefit from it.
* Your client began the assignment, but gave up soon after when he realised that he did not know what to do. This happens particularly with written ABC homework assignments.
* Your client began the assignment, but encountered a critical A which triggered a new undiscovered irrational belief which led him to abandon the assignment.

Let's look at how I responded to Norman when he reported a homework 'failure'.

Windy: Let's start by considering your homework. How did it go?

Norman: Not very well.

Windy: I'm sorry to hear that. Tell me what happened.

[Here, I begin by asking for a factual account of Norman's experience with the assignment.]

Norman: Well, before the first seminar, I practised the rational beliefs that we discussed and was all geared up to speak up. So after about ten minutes I spoke up, but it didn't go too well. So I didn't do it again.

Windy: Now, do you remember the concept of the 'no-lose' homework assignment?

Norman: I think so. it means that if I do the assignment and it works out, that's fine. And it is also valuable if I do it and it doesn't work out well; that's also valuable because we can discover why.

Windy: Good. Now, let's see if we can discover why in your case. Let me start by asking you what rational beliefs you practised before speaking up at the first seminar.

[Norman's report indicated that he practised the correct rational beliefs and did so with sufficient force.]

Windy: Well that seems fine. Now let's look closely at what happened when you spoke up at the first seminar.

Norman: Well, there was a gap in the conversation so I went over the rational beliefs again and took the plunge and spoke up.

Windy: And what happened?

Norman: Well, I wasn't too anxious while I was speaking. But when I stopped I got a bit depressed.

Windy: What were you most depressed about?

[Here I am attempting to identify Norman's critical A (see Dryden, 1995). It transpired that Norman was depressed about not saying something particularly noteworthy. His irrational belief was 'When I speak up in class, I must say something noteworthy and if I don't then I am something of a failure.' I then helped Norman to challenge and change this irrational belief.]

Windy: So, Norman, can you now see why you got depressed about what you said and why you didn't speak up in the subsequent two seminars?

Norman: Yes, I can. That's really helpful. I can now really see what you meant by the 'no-lose' homework assignment.

Windy: That's really good. Now let me suggest that you do the same homework between now and next week, but this time how about practising the new rational belief as well, namely: 'I would like to say something noteworthy every time I speak up in class, but I don't have to do so. If I don't, I'm not a failure. Rather I am a fallible human being who says noteworthy and mundane things at times?'

Norman: That's a good idea.

[I then take Norman through an imagery assignment to give him some practice at the new rational belief, after which we both make a written note of his new assignment.]

Unit 63: Dealing with the situation when your client has not done the homework assignment

Despite the fact that you may have taken the utmost care in negotiating a homework assignment with your client and instituted all the safeguards that I discussed in Module 11, your client may still not carry it out. When this happens, I suggest that you follow a similar procedure that I discussed in the previous unit; that is, ask your client for a factual account of the situation where she contracted to do the assignment but didn't do it, remind him of the 'no-lose' concept of homework assignments, identify and deal with the factors that accounted for him not doing the assignment and then re-negotiate the same or similar assignment. As you investigate the aforementioned factors, be particularly aware of the fact that you may have failed to institute one or more of the safeguards reviewed in the previous module. If this is the case and your failure to do so accounts for your client not carrying out the assignment, then take responsibility for this omission, disclose this to your client, institute the safeguard and re-negotiate the assignment.

On the other hand, if the reason why your client did not do the assignment can be attributed to a factor in the client that you could not have foreseen, help him to deal with it and again re-negotiate the same or similar assignment.

In investigating the reason why Norman did not carry out his homework, it transpired that he did not do so because he believed that he had to feel comfortable before speaking up. Team up with a trainee colleague, play the role of therapist and have him or her play Norman and see if you can help your 'client' over the obstacle and then re-negotiate the same homework assignment. Tape record the interchange and play the recording to your REBT trainer or supervisor for feedback.

Appendix 2 contains a form that I recommend you use with your clients when they consistently fail to initiate negotiated homework assignments. I suggest that you use this form in training as well. Again pair up with a trainee colleague and have him or her play the role of a client who doesn't do homework assignments for each of the reasons shown on the form and gain practice at helping your 'client' over the obstacle. Tape record the interchanges and once again seek feedback from your REBT trainer or supervisor.

We have now reached the end of this, the second of the volumes in the 'Practical Skills in Rational Emotive Behaviour Therapy' series. In the next volume in the series I present verbatim transcripts, with commentary, of REBT demonstration sessions of the kind that are regularly conducted by REBT trainers during training courses. I hope that these 'full' sessions with accompanying commentary will give you a sense of how REBT sessions unfold and will demonstrate how the skills that I have discussed in this and the previous volume in the series (Dryden, 1995) can be integrated in the course of an entire session.

Appendix 1

Homework Skills Monitoring Form

Listen to the audiotape of your therapy session and circle 'Yes', 'No' or 'N/A' (Not Appropriate) for each item. For every item circled 'No', write down in the space provided what you would have done differently given hindsight and what you would have needed to change in order to have circled the item 'Yes'.

1. Did I use a term for homework assignments that was acceptable to the client?

Yes   No   N/A

2. Did I properly negotiate the homework assignment with the client (as opposed to telling him/her what to do or accepting uncritically his/her suggestion)?

Yes   No   N/A

3. Was the homework assignment expressed clearly?

Yes   No   N/A

4. Did I ensure that the client understood the homework assignment?

Yes   No   N/A

5. Was the homework assignment relevant to my client's therapy goals?

Yes   No   N/A

6. Did I help the client understand the relevance of the homework assignment to his/her therapy goals?

Yes   No   N/A

7. Did the homework assignment follow logically from the work I did with the client in the session?

Yes   No   N/A

8. Was the type of homework assignment I negotiated with the client relevant to the stage reached by the two of us on his/her target problem?

Yes   No   N/A

9. Did I employ the 'challenging, but not overwhelming' principle in negotiating the homework assignment?

Yes   No   N/A

10: Did I introduce and explain the 'no lose' concept of homework assignments?

Yes   No   N/A

11. Did I ensure that the client had the necessary skills to carry out the homework assignment?

Yes   No   N/A

12. Did I ensure that the client believed that he/she could do the homework assignment?

Yes   No   N/A

13. Did I allow sufficient time in the session to negotiate the homework assignment properly?

Yes   No   N/A

14. Did I elicit a firm commitment from the client that he/she would carry out the homework assignment?

Yes   No   N/A

15. Did I help the client to specify when, where and how often he/she would carry out the homework assignment?

Yes   No   N/A

16. Did I encourage my client to make a written note of the homework assignment and its relevant details?

Yes   No   N/A

17. Did the client and I both retain a copy of this written note?

Yes   No   N/A

18. Did I elicit from the client potential obstacles to homework completion?

Yes   No   N/A

19. Did I help the client to deal in advance with any potential obstacles that he/she disclosed?

Yes   No   N/A

20. Did I help the client to rehearse the homework assignment in the session?

Yes   No   N/A

21. Did I use the principle of rewards and penalties with the client?

Yes   No   N/A

Appendix 2

Possible Reasons for not Doing Self-help Assignments

(To be Completed by Clients)

The following is a list of reasons that various clients have given for not doing their self-help assignments during the course of counselling. Because the speed of improvement depends primarily on the amount of self-help assignments that you are willing to do, it is of great importance to pinpoint any reasons that you may have for not doing this work. It is important to look for these reasons at the time that you feel a reluctance to do your assignment or a desire to put off doing it. Hence, it is best to fill out this questionnaire at that time. If you have any difficulty filling out this form and returning it to the counsellor, it might be best to do it together during a counselling session. (Rate each statement by ringing 'T' (True) 'F' (False). 'T' indicates that you agree with it; 'F' means the statement does not apply at this time.)

1. It seems that nothing can help me so there is no point in trying.   T/F
2. It wasn't clear, I didn't understand what I had to do.   T/F
3. I thought that the particular method the counsellor had suggested would not be helpful. I didn't really see the value of it.   T/F
4. It seemed too hard.   T/F
5. I am willing to do self-help assignments, but I keep forgetting.   T/F
6. I did not have enough time. I was too busy.   T/F
7. If I do something the counsellor suggests I do it's not as good as if I come up with my own ideas.   T/F
8. I don't really believe I can do anything to help myself.   T/F
9. I have the impression the counsellor is trying to boss me around or control me.   T/F
10. I worry about the counsellor's disapproval. I believe that what I do just won't be good enough for him/her.   T/F
11. I felt too bad, sad, nervous, upset (underline the appropriate word(s)) to do it.   T/F
12. I would have found doing the homework assignment too upsetting.   T/F
13. It was too much to do.   T/F
14. It's too much like going back to school again.   T/F
15. It seemed to be mainly for the counsellor's benefit.   T/F
16. Self-help assignments have no place in counselling.   T/F
17. Because of the progress I've made these assignments are likely to be of no further benefit to me.   T/F
18. Because these assignments have not been helpful in the past, I couldn't see the point of doing this one.   T/F
19. I don't agree with this particular approach to counselling.   T/F
20. OTHER REASONS (please write them).

Appendix 3

Training in Rational Emotive Behaviour Therapy

1. For further details of training courses in REBT in Britain, contact:
   Centre for REBT
   156 Westcombe Hill
   Blackheath
   London
   SE3 7DX
   Tel: (0181) 293 4114

2. For further details of training courses in REBT worldwide, contact:
   Director of Professional Education
   Institute for RET
   45 East 65th Street
   New York
   NY 10021
   USA
   Tel: 0101 212 535 0822

References

Bandura, A. (1977). *Social Learning Theory*. Englewood Cliffs, NJ: Prentice-Hall.

Beck, A.T., Rush, A.J., Shaw, B.F. & Emery, G. (1979). *Cognitive Therapy of Depression*. New York: Guilford.

Bordin, E. S. (1979). The generalizability of the psychoanalytic concept of the working alliance. *Psychotherapy: Theory, Research and Practice* 16, 252–260.

DiGiuseppe, R. (1991). Comprehensive cognitive disputing in rational emotive therapy. In M. Bernard (Ed.), *Using Rational-emotive Therapy Effectively*. New York: Plenum.

Dryden, W. (1987). *Current Issues in Rational-emotive Therapy*. Beckenham, Kent: Croom Helm.

Dryden, W. (1988). Language and meaning in rational-emotive therapy. In W. Dryden & P. Trower (Eds), *Developments in Rational-emotive Therapy*. Milton Keynes: Open University Press.

Dryden, W. (Ed.) (1989). Howard Young – Rational Therapist: Seminal Papers in Rational-emotive Therapy. Loughton, Essex: Gale Centre Publications.

Dryden, W. (1991). *Reason and Therapeutic Change*. London: Whurr Publishers.

Dryden, W. (1992). *The Incredible Sulk*. London: Sheldon.

Dryden, W. (1994a). *Ten Steps to Positive Living*. London: Sheldon.

Dryden, W. (1994b). *Invitation to Rational-emotive Psychology*. London: Whurr Publishers.

Dryden, W. (1994c). *Overcoming Guilt*. London: Sheldon.

Dryden, W. (1995). *Preparing for Client Change in Rational Emotive Behaviour Therapy*. London: Whurr Publishers.

Dryden, W. & Gordon, J. (1990). Think Your Way to Happiness. London: Sheldon.

Dryden, W. & Gordon, J. (1992). *Think Rationally: A Brief Guide to Overcoming your Emotional Problems*. London: Centre for Rational Emotive Therapy.

Dryden, W. & Gordon, J. (1993). Beating the Comfort Trap. London: Sheldon.

Ellis, A. (1963). Toward a more precise definition of 'emotional' and 'intellectual' insight. *Psychological Reports*, 23, 538–540.

Ellis, A. (1976). The biological basis of human irrationality. *Journal of Individual Psychology*, 32, 145–168.

Ellis, A. (1983). The philosophic implications and dangers of some popular behavior therapy techniques. In M. Rosenbaum, C.M. Franks & Y. Jaffe (Eds), *Perspectives in Behavior Therapy in the Eighties*. New York: Springer.

Ellis, A. (1985). *Overcoming Resistance: Rational-emotive Therapy with Difficult Clients*. New York: Springer.

Ellis, A. & Dryden, W. (1987). *The Practice of Rational-emotive Therapy*. New York: Springer.

Ellis, A. & Harper, R.A. (1975). A New Guide to Rational Living. Hollywood, CA: Wilshire.

Golden, W.L. (1989). Resistance and change in cognitive-behaviour therapy. In W. Dryden & P. Trower (Eds), *Cognitive Psychotherapy: Stasis and Change*. London: Cassell.

Hauck, P. (1974). *Depression: Why it Happens and How to Overcome it*. London: Sheldon.

Hauck, P. (1980). Calm Down: How to Cope with Frustration and Anger. London: Sheldon.

Hauck, P. (1981a). *How to Stand up for Yourself*. London: Sheldon.

Hauck, P. (1981b). *Why be Afraid?* London: Sheldon.

Hauck. P. (1991). *Hold your Head up High*. London: Sheldon.

Mahrer, A. R. (Ed.). (1967). *The Goals of Psychotherapy*. New York: Appleton-Century-Crofts.

Maluccio, A.N. (1979). *Learning from Clients: Interpersonal Helping as Viewed by Clients and Social Workers*. New York: Free Press.

Segal, J. (1993). *Against self-disclosure. In W. Dryden (Ed.),* Questions and Answers on Counselling in Action. London: Sage.

Walen, S.R., DiGiuseppe, R. & Dryden, W. (1992). *A Practitioner's Guide to Rational-emotive Therapy*, second edition. New York: Oxford University Press.

Yankura. J. & Dryden, W. (1990). *Doing RET: Albert Ellis in Action*. New York: Springer.

Young, H.S. (1974). *A Rational Counseling Primer*. New York: Institute for Rational-Emotive Therapy.

Index